Text-Based Writing Nonfiction

Grade 5

The following photos and images were provided through Shutterstock.com and are protected by copyright:
Muellek Josef, picturepartners (page 14); DenisNata (page 15); photosync (pages 24, 25); Eastimages, Jessmine (page 35); OHishiapply (page 64); Africa Studio (page 75); MariusdeGraf (page 94); paulista, stocksolutions, Mariyana Misaleva, Jacek Chabraszewski (page 95); Vadim Petrakov (page 105); lukeruk (page 124); ducu59us (page 125)

The remaining photos and images were provided by the organizations and individuals listed below and are also protected by copyright:
United States Department of Agriculture (page 44); Collection of the Supreme Court of the United States, Steve Petteway (page 54); Ipankonin (page 55); Franz Haag, Harry Shipler (page 65); Donna Coveney/MIT (page 74); Monterey Bay Aquarium (page 85); Dr. Paula Kahumbu/WildlifeDirect (page 104)

Writing: Carrie Gwynne
Editorial Development: Renee Biermann
Lisa Vitarisi Mathews
Copy Editing: Cathy Harber
Art Direction: Cheryl Puckett
Art Management: Kathy Kopp
Cover Design: Yuki Meyer
Cover Illustration: Chris Vallo
Design/Production: Susan Lovell
Jessica Onken

EMC 6035

Evan-Moor®
Helping Children Learn

Visit
teaching-standards.com
to view a correlation
of this book.
This is a free service.

**Correlated to State and
Common Core State Standards**

**Congratulations on your purchase of some of the
finest teaching materials in the world.**

*Photocopying the pages in this book
is permitted for <u>single-classroom use only</u>.
Making photocopies for additional classes
or schools is prohibited.*

Contents

What's in Every Unit?

For the Teacher

Resource pages outline lesson objectives and provide instructional guidance.

The reading level helps identify appropriate texts.

Lesson objectives and content-area concepts are indicated.

Common Core State Standards correlations are located in each unit for easy reference.

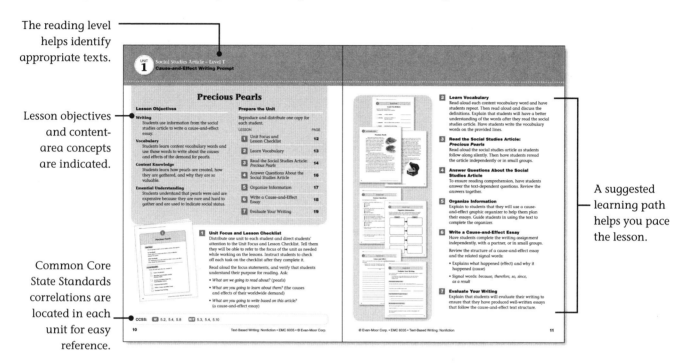

A suggested learning path helps you pace the lesson.

For the Student

Student pages provide unit focus, organizational tools, nonfiction content, and skills practice.

1 Unit Focus and Lesson Checklist

The Unit Focus provides a purpose for reading.

The Lesson Checklist guides students through the learning path.

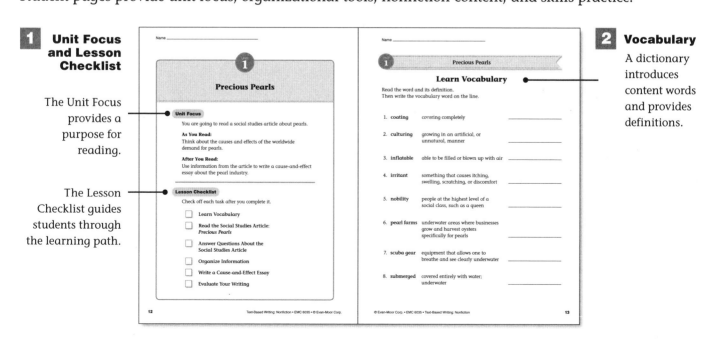

2 Vocabulary

A dictionary introduces content words and provides definitions.

3 **Nonfiction Article**

A two-page article introduces a content-area topic and provides details.

Illustrations and graphics provide additional information and context.

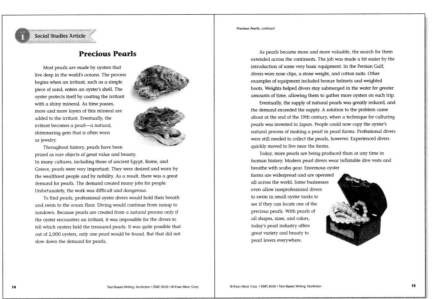

4 **Comprehension Questions**

Text-based questions appear in multiple-choice and constructed-response formats.

5 **Graphic Organizer**

A graphic organizer helps students organize information from the article to plan their writing.

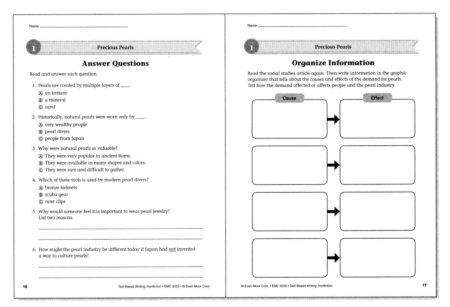

6 **Writing Prompt**

A text-based writing prompt helps students synthesize what they've learned.

7 **Writing Evaluation**

A review of nonfiction writing structures guides students in evaluating their essay.

Correlations:
Common Core State Standards

	Units					
	1	**2**	**3**	**4**	**5**	**6**
W Writing Standards for Grade 5	Precious Pearls	Beef or Bugs?	Building a Better Nest	Fabulous Foods	Sonia Sotomayor	Transportation Over Time
Text Types and Purposes						
5.1 Write opinion pieces on topics or texts, supporting a point of view with reasons and information. **a.** Introduce a topic or text clearly, state an opinion, and create an organizational structure in which ideas are logically grouped to support the writer's purpose. **b.** Provide logically ordered reasons that are supported by facts and details.						
5.2 Write informative/explanatory texts to examine a topic and convey ideas and information clearly.	●	●	●	●	●	●
Production and Distribution of Writing						
5.4 Produce clear and coherent writing in which the development and organization are appropriate to task, purpose, and audience. (Grade-specific expectations for writing types are defined in standards 1 and 2 above.)	●	●	●	●	●	●
Research to Build and Present Knowledge						
5.8 Recall relevant information from experiences or gather relevant information from print and digital sources; summarize or paraphrase information in notes and finished work; and provide a list of sources.	●	●	●	●	●	●
RIT Reading Standards for Informational Text, Grade 5						
Key Ideas and Details						
5.3 Explain the relationships or interactions between two or more individuals, events, ideas, or concepts in a historical, scientific, or technical text based on specific information in the text.	●	●	●	●	●	●
Craft and Structure						
5.4 Determine the meaning of general academic and domain-specific words and phrases in a text relevant to a *grade 5 topic or subject area*.	●	●	●	●	●	●
Range of Reading and Level of Text Complexity						
5.10 By the end of year, read and comprehend informational texts, including history/social studies, science, and technical texts, in the grades 4–5 text complexity band proficiently, with scaffolding as needed at the high end of the range.	●	●	●	●	●	●

Units						
7	8	9	10	11	12
Paula Hammond	A Matter of Facts	May I Take Your Order?	Lion Lights	One Nation, One Language?	Simple Treats

W Writing Standards for Grade 5

Text Types and Purposes

7	8	9	10	11	12	
●	●	●	●	●	●	**5.1** Write opinion pieces on topics or texts, supporting a point of view with reasons and information. a. Introduce a topic or text clearly, state an opinion, and create an organizational structure in which ideas are logically grouped to support the writer's purpose. b. Provide logically ordered reasons that are supported by facts and details.
						5.2 Write informative/explanatory texts to examine a topic and convey ideas and information clearly.

Production and Distribution of Writing

7	8	9	10	11	12	
●	●	●	●	●	●	**5.4** Produce clear and coherent writing in which the development and organization are appropriate to task, purpose, and audience. (Grade-specific expectations for writing types are defined in standards 1 and 2 above.)

Research to Build and Present Knowledge

7	8	9	10	11	12	
●	●	●	●	●	●	**5.8** Recall relevant information from experiences or gather relevant information from print and digital sources; summarize or paraphrase information in notes and finished work; and provide a list of sources.

RIT Reading Standards for Informational Text, Grade 5

Key Ideas and Details

7	8	9	10	11	12	
●	●	●	●	●	●	**5.3** Explain the relationships or interactions between two or more individuals, events, ideas, or concepts in a historical, scientific, or technical text based on specific information in the text.

Craft and Structure

7	8	9	10	11	12	
●	●	●	●	●	●	**5.4** Determine the meaning of general academic and domain-specific words and phrases in a text relevant to a *grade 5 topic or subject area*.

Range of Reading and Level of Text Complexity

7	8	9	10	11	12	
●	●	●	●	●	●	**5.10** By the end of year, read and comprehend informational texts, including history/social studies, science, and technical texts, in the grades 4–5 text complexity band proficiently, with scaffolding as needed at the high end of the range.

Correlations:
Texas Essential Knowledge and Skills

	Units				
	1	2	3	4	5
110.13 English Language Arts and Reading, Grade 5	Precious Pearls	Beef or Bugs?	Building a Better Nest	Fabulous Foods	Sonia Sotomayor
Writing					
(15) Writing/Writing Process. Students use elements of the writing process (planning, drafting, revising, editing, and publishing) to compose text. Students are expected to:	●	●	●	●	●
(A) plan a first draft by selecting a genre appropriate for conveying the intended meaning to an audience, determine appropriate topics through a range of strategies (e.g., discussion, background reading, personal interests, interviews), and develop a thesis or controlling idea.	●	●	●	●	●
(18) Writing/Expository and Procedural Texts. Students write expository and procedural or work-related texts to communicate ideas and information to specific audiences for specific purposes. Students are expected to:	●	●	●	●	●
(C) write responses to literary or expository texts and provide evidence from the text to demonstrate understanding.	●	●	●	●	●
(19) Writing/Persuasive Texts. Students write persuasive texts to influence the attitudes or actions of a specific audience on specific issues. Students are expected to write persuasive essays for appropriate audiences that establish a position and include sound reasoning, detailed and relevant evidence, and consideration of alternatives.					
Reading					
(11) Reading/Comprehension of Informational Text/Expository Text. Students analyze, make inferences, and draw conclusions about expository text and provide evidence from text to support their understanding. Students are expected to:	●	●	●	●	●
(C) analyze how the organizational pattern of a text (e.g., cause-and-effect, compare-and-contrast, sequential order, logical order, classification schemes) influences the relationships among the ideas, and	●	●		●	●
(D) use multiple text features and graphics to gain an overview of the contents of text and to locate information.	●	●	●	●	
(13) Reading/Comprehension of Informational Text/Procedural Texts. Students understand how to glean and use information in procedural texts and documents. Students are expected to:				●	
(A) interpret details from procedural text to complete a task, solve a problem, or perform procedures, and				●	
(B) interpret factual or quantitative information presented in maps, charts, illustrations, graphs, timelines, tables, and diagrams.				●	

Text-Based Writing: Nonfiction • EMC 6035 • © Evan-Moor Corp.

			Units			
6	7	8	9	10	11	12
Transportation Over Time	Paula Hammond	A Matter of Facts	May I Take Your Order?	Lion Lights	One Nation, One Language?	Simple Treats
•	•	•	•	•	•	•
•	•	•	•	•	•	•
•						
•	•	•	•	•	•	•
	•	•	•	•	•	•
•	•	•	•	•	•	•
•	•	•	•	•	•	•
•		•	•		•	
		•				
		•				
		•				

Precious Pearls

Lesson Objectives

Writing
Students use information from the social studies article to write a cause-and-effect essay.

Vocabulary
Students learn content vocabulary words and use those words to write about the causes and effects of the demand for pearls.

Content Knowledge
Students learn how pearls are created, how they are gathered, and why they are so valuable.

Essential Understanding
Students understand that pearls were and are expensive because they are rare and hard to gather and are used to indicate social status.

Prepare the Unit

Reproduce and distribute one copy for each student.

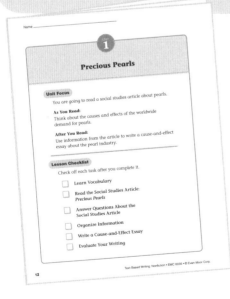

1 Unit Focus and Lesson Checklist

Distribute one unit to each student and direct students' attention to the Unit Focus and Lesson Checklist. Tell them they will be able to refer to the focus of the unit as needed while working on the lessons. Instruct students to check off each task on the checklist after they complete it.

Read aloud the focus statements, and verify that students understand their purpose for reading. Ask:

- *What are we going to read about?* (pearls)

- *What are you going to learn about them?* (the causes and effects of their worldwide demand)

- *What are you going to write based on this article?* (a cause-and-effect essay)

CCSS: **W** 5.2, 5.4, 5.8 **RIT** 5.3, 5.4, 5.10

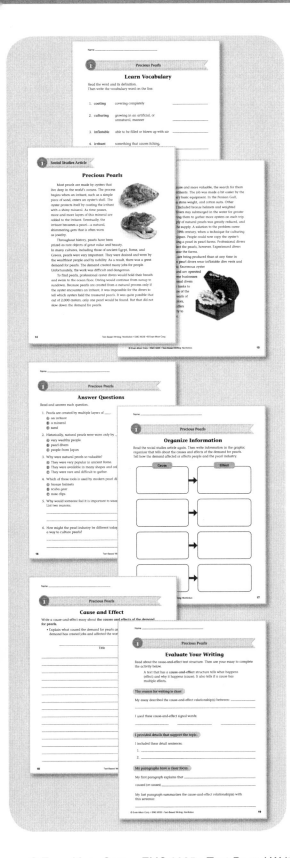

2 Learn Vocabulary

Read aloud each content vocabulary word and have students repeat. Then read aloud and discuss the definitions. Explain that students will have a better understanding of the words after they read the social studies article. Have students write the vocabulary words on the provided lines.

3 Read the Social Studies Article: *Precious Pearls*

Read aloud the social studies article as students follow along silently. Then have students reread the article independently or in small groups.

4 Answer Questions About the Social Studies Article

To ensure reading comprehension, have students answer the text-dependent questions. Review the answers together.

5 Organize Information

Explain to students that they will use a cause-and-effect graphic organizer to help them plan their essays. Guide students in using the text to complete the organizer.

6 Write a Cause-and-Effect Essay

Have students complete the writing assignment independently, with a partner, or in small groups.

Review the structure of a cause-and-effect essay and the related signal words:

• Explains what happened (effect) and why it happened (cause)

• Signal words: *because, therefore, so, since, as a result*

7 Evaluate Your Writing

Explain that students will evaluate their writing to ensure that they have produced well-written essays that follow the cause-and-effect text structure.

UNIT
1

Precious Pearls

Unit Focus

You are going to read a social studies article about pearls.

As You Read:

Think about the causes and effects of the worldwide demand for pearls.

After You Read:

Use information from the article to write a cause-and-effect essay about the pearl industry.

Lesson Checklist

Check off each task after you complete it.

☐ **Learn Vocabulary**

☐ **Read the Social Studies Article:** *Precious Pearls*

☐ **Answer Questions About the Social Studies Article**

☐ **Organize Information**

☐ **Write a Cause-and-Effect Essay**

☐ **Evaluate Your Writing**

Precious Pearls

Learn Vocabulary

Read the word and its definition.
Then write the vocabulary word on the line.

1. **coating**   covering completely   _____

2. **culturing**   growing in an artificial, or
unnatural, manner   _____

3. **inflatable**   able to be filled or blown up with air   _____

4. **irritant**   something that causes itching,
swelling, scratching, or discomfort   _____

5. **nobility**   people at the highest level of a
social class, such as a queen   _____

6. **pearl farms**   underwater areas where businesses
grow and harvest oysters
specifically for pearls   _____

7. **scuba gear**   equipment that allows one to
breathe and see clearly underwater   _____

8. **submerged**   covered entirely with water;
underwater   _____

Precious Pearls

Most pearls are made by oysters that live deep in the world's oceans. The process begins when an irritant, such as a simple piece of sand, enters an oyster's shell. The oyster protects itself by coating the irritant with a shiny mineral. As time passes, more and more layers of this mineral are added to the irritant. Eventually, the irritant becomes a pearl—a natural, shimmering gem that is often worn as jewelry.

Throughout history, pearls have been prized as rare objects of great value and beauty. In many cultures, including those of ancient Egypt, Rome, and Greece, pearls were very important. They were desired and worn by the wealthiest people and by nobility. As a result, there was a great demand for pearls. The demand created many jobs for people. Unfortunately, the work was difficult and dangerous.

To find pearls, professional oyster divers would hold their breath and swim to the ocean floor. Diving would continue from sunup to sundown. Because pearls are created from a natural process only if the oyster encounters an irritant, it was impossible for the divers to tell which oysters held the treasured pearls. It was quite possible that out of 2,000 oysters, only one pearl would be found. But that did not slow down the demand for pearls.

As pearls became more and more valuable, the search for them extended across the continents. The job was made a bit easier by the introduction of some very basic equipment. In the Persian Gulf, divers wore nose clips, a stone weight, and cotton suits. Other examples of equipment included bronze helmets and weighted boots. Weights helped divers stay submerged in the water for greater amounts of time, allowing them to gather more oysters on each trip.

Eventually, the supply of natural pearls was greatly reduced, and the demand exceeded the supply. A solution to the problem came about at the end of the 19th century, when a technique for culturing pearls was invented in Japan. People could now copy the oyster's natural process of making a pearl in pearl farms. Professional divers were still needed to collect the pearls, however. Experienced divers quickly moved to live near the farms.

Today, more pearls are being produced than at any time in human history. Modern pearl divers wear inflatable dive vests and breathe with scuba gear. Enormous oyster farms are widespread and are operated all across the world. Some businesses even allow nonprofessional divers to swim in small oyster tanks to see if they can locate one of the precious pearls. With pearls of all shapes, sizes, and colors, today's pearl industry offers great variety and beauty to pearl lovers everywhere.

Precious Pearls

Answer Questions

Read and answer each question.

1. Pearls are created by multiple layers of ____.

   Ⓐ an irritant

   Ⓑ a mineral

   Ⓒ sand

2. Historically, natural pearls were worn only by ____.

   Ⓐ very wealthy people

   Ⓑ pearl divers

   Ⓒ people from Japan

3. Why were natural pearls so valuable?

   Ⓐ They were very popular in ancient Rome.

   Ⓑ They were available in many shapes and colors.

   Ⓒ They were rare and difficult to gather.

4. Which of these tools is used by modern pearl divers?

   Ⓐ bronze helmets

   Ⓑ scuba gear

   Ⓒ nose clips

5. Why would someone feel it is important to wear pearl jewelry?
   List two reasons.

   _____

   _____

6. How might the pearl industry be different today if Japan had <u>not</u> invented
   a way to culture pearls?

   _____

   _____

Name _____

Organize Information

Read the social studies article again. Then write information in the graphic organizer that tells about the causes and effects of the demand for pearls. Tell how the demand affected or affects people and the pearl industry.

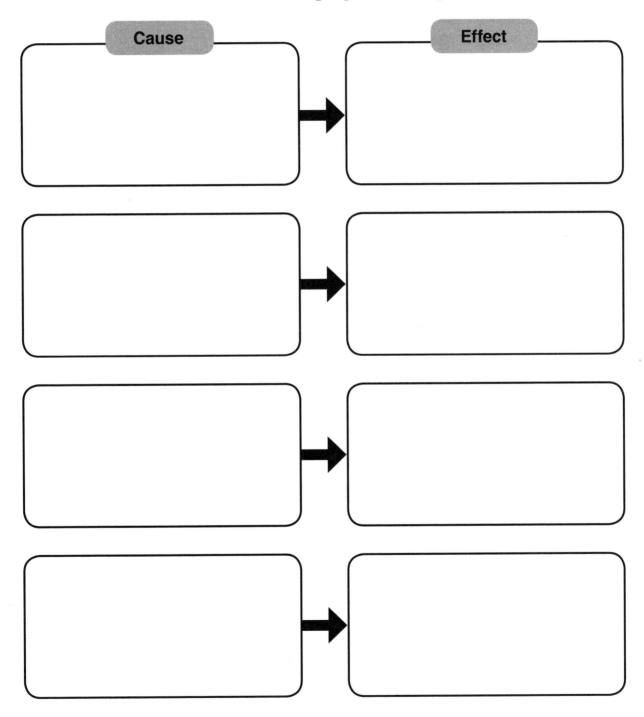

Cause

Effect

Name _____

Cause and Effect

Write a cause-and-effect essay about **the causes and effects of the demand for pearls**.

- Explain what caused the demand for pearls and how that demand has created jobs and affected the world.

_____
Title

_____

_____

_____

_____

_____

_____

_____

_____

_____

_____

_____

_____

Name _____

Evaluate Your Writing

Read about the cause-and-effect text structure. Then use your essay to complete the activity below.

> A text that has a **cause-and-effect** structure tells what happens (effect) and why it happens (cause). It also tells if a cause has multiple effects.

The reason for writing is clear.

My essay described the cause-and-effect relationship(s) between: _____

_____

I used these cause-and-effect signal words:

_____   _____   _____

I provided details that support the topic.

I included these detail sentences:

1. _____

2. _____

My paragraphs have a clear focus.

My first paragraph explains that _____

caused (or causes) _____

My last paragraph summarizes the cause-and-effect relationship(s) with this sentence:

_____

Beef or Bugs?

Lesson Objectives

Writing
Students use information from the science article to write a cause-and-effect essay.

Vocabulary
Students learn content vocabulary words and use those words to write about how eating insects instead of beef could help the atmosphere.

Content Knowledge
Students learn about the benefits of eating insects and how methane gas affects the atmosphere.

Essential Understanding
Students understand that people around the world eat insects as part of their regular diet and that humans must work together to keep Earth safe.

Prepare the Unit

Reproduce and distribute one copy for each student.

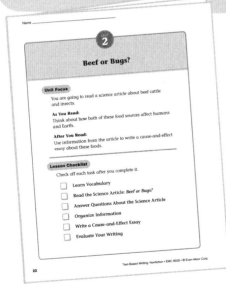

1 Unit Focus and Lesson Checklist

Distribute one unit to each student and direct students' attention to the Unit Focus and Lesson Checklist. Tell them they will be able to refer to the focus of the unit as needed while working on the lessons. Instruct students to check off each task on the checklist after they complete it.

Read aloud the focus statements, and verify that students understand their purpose for reading. Ask:

- *What are we going to read about?* (beef cattle and insects)

- *What are you going to learn about them?* (how they affect Earth)

- *What are you going to write based on this article?* (a cause-and-effect essay)

CCSS: **W** 5.2, 5.4, 5.8   **RIT** 5.3, 5.4, 5.10

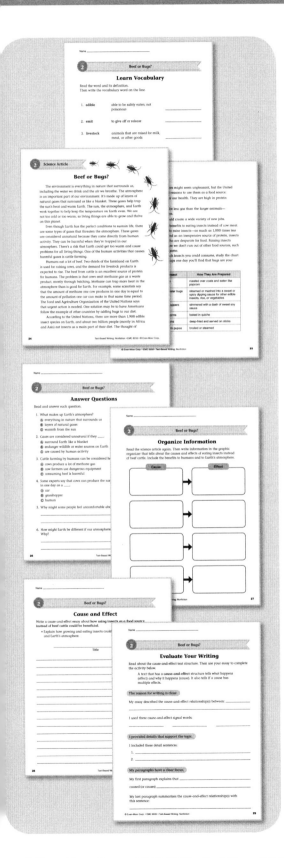

2 Learn Vocabulary
Read aloud each content vocabulary word and have students repeat. Then read aloud and discuss the definitions. Explain that students will have a better understanding of the words after they read the science article. Have students write the vocabulary words on the provided lines.

3 Read the Science Article: *Beef or Bugs?*
Read aloud the science article as students follow along silently. Then have students reread the article independently or in small groups.

4 Answer Questions About the Science Article
To ensure reading comprehension, have students answer the text-dependent questions. Review the answers together.

5 Organize Information
Explain to students that they will use a cause-and-effect graphic organizer to help them plan their essays. Guide students in using the text to complete the organizer.

6 Write a Cause-and-Effect Essay
Have students complete the writing assignment independently, with a partner, or in small groups.

Review the structure of a cause-and-effect essay and the related signal words:

- Explains what happened (effect) and why it happened (cause)

- Signal words: *because, therefore, so, since, as a result*

7 Evaluate Your Writing
Explain that students will evaluate their writing to ensure that they have produced well-written essays that follow the cause-and-effect text structure.

UNIT 2

Beef or Bugs?

Unit Focus

You are going to read a science article about beef cattle and insects.

As You Read:

Think about how both of these food sources affect humans and Earth.

After You Read:

Use information from the article to write a cause-and-effect essay about these foods.

Lesson Checklist

Check off each task after you complete it.

- [ ] **Learn Vocabulary**
- [ ] **Read the Science Article: *Beef or Bugs?***
- [ ] **Answer Questions About the Science Article**
- [ ] **Organize Information**
- [ ] **Write a Cause-and-Effect Essay**
- [ ] **Evaluate Your Writing**

UNIT 2

Learn Vocabulary

Read the word and its definition.
Then write the vocabulary word on the line.

1. **edible**   able to be safely eaten; not poisonous   _____

2. **emit**   to give off or release   _____

3. **livestock**   animals that are raised for milk, meat, or other goods   _____

4. **pollution**   harmful materials such as certain gases, chemicals, and waste released into the air or ground through human acts or by animals   _____

5. **sustain**   to keep something going; to repeat an action   _____

6. **thrive**   to live well; to be healthy and happy   _____

7. **wild game**   wild animals hunted for food, such as deer or pheasants   _____

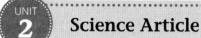

Beef or Bugs?

The environment is everything in nature that surrounds us, including the water we drink and the air we breathe. The atmosphere is an important part of our environment. It's made up of layers of natural gases that surround us like a blanket. These gases help trap the sun's heat and warm Earth. The sun, the atmosphere, and Earth work together to help keep the temperature on Earth even. We are not too cold or too warm, so living things are able to grow and thrive on this planet.

Even though Earth has the perfect conditions to sustain life, there are some types of gases that threaten the atmosphere. These gases are considered unnatural because they come directly from human activity. They can be harmful when they're trapped in our atmosphere. There's a risk that Earth could get too warm and cause problems for all living things. One of the human activities that causes harmful gases is cattle farming.

Humans eat a lot of beef. Two-thirds of the farmland on Earth is used for raising cows, and the demand for livestock products is expected to rise. The beef from cattle is an excellent source of protein for humans. The problem is that cows emit methane gas as a waste product, mostly through belching. Methane can trap more heat in the atmosphere than is good for Earth. For example, some scientists say that the amount of methane one cow produces in one day is equal to the amount of pollution one car can make in that same time period. The Food and Agriculture Organization of the United Nations says that urgent action is needed. One solution may be to have Americans follow the example of other countries by adding bugs to our diet.

According to the United Nations, there are more than 1,900 edible insect species on Earth, and about two billion people (mostly in Africa and Asia) eat insects as a main part of their diet. The thought of eating these little creatures might seem unpleasant, but the United Nations gives three good reasons to use them as a food source:

- Insects are good for our health. They are high in protein and calcium.

- Insects produce a lot less gas than the larger animals— about 100 times less.

- Insect farming would create a wide variety of new jobs.

There are also other benefits to eating insects instead of cow meat. It takes much less water to raise insects—as much as 1,000 times less than raising livestock. And as an inexpensive source of protein, insects could help feed people who are desperate for food. Raising insects would also help make sure we don't run out of other food sources, such as sea creatures or wild game.

For some idea of which insects you could consume, study the chart below. Who knows? Perhaps one day you'll find that bugs are your favorite snack!

Location	Insect	How They Are Prepared
Amazon basin; Africa	beetles	roasted over coals and eaten like popcorn
Asia	giant water bugs	steamed or mashed into a sweet or spicy dipping sauce for other edible insects, rice, or vegetables
Japan	grasshoppers	simmered with a dash of sweet soy sauce
Netherlands	mealworms	baked in quiche
China	scorpions	deep-fried and served on sticks
South Korea	silkworm pupae	broiled or steamed

Beef or Bugs?

Answer Questions

Read and answer each question.

1. What makes up Earth's atmosphere?

    Ⓐ everything in nature that surrounds us

    Ⓑ layers of natural gases

    Ⓒ warmth from the sun

2. Gases are considered unnatural if they ____.

    Ⓐ surround Earth like a blanket

    Ⓑ endanger wildlife or water sources on Earth

    Ⓒ are caused by human activity

3. Cattle farming by humans can be considered harmful because ____.

    Ⓐ cows produce a lot of methane gas

    Ⓑ cow farmers use dangerous equipment

    Ⓒ consuming beef is harmful

4. Some experts say that cows can produce the same amount of methane in one day as a ____.

    Ⓐ car

    Ⓑ grasshopper

    Ⓒ human

5. Why might some people feel uncomfortable about eating insects?

    _____

    _____

6. How might Earth be different if our atmosphere was too hot or too cold? Why?

    _____

    _____

Organize Information

Read the science article again. Then write information in the graphic organizer that tells about the causes and effects of eating insects instead of beef cattle. Include the benefits to humans and to Earth's atmosphere.

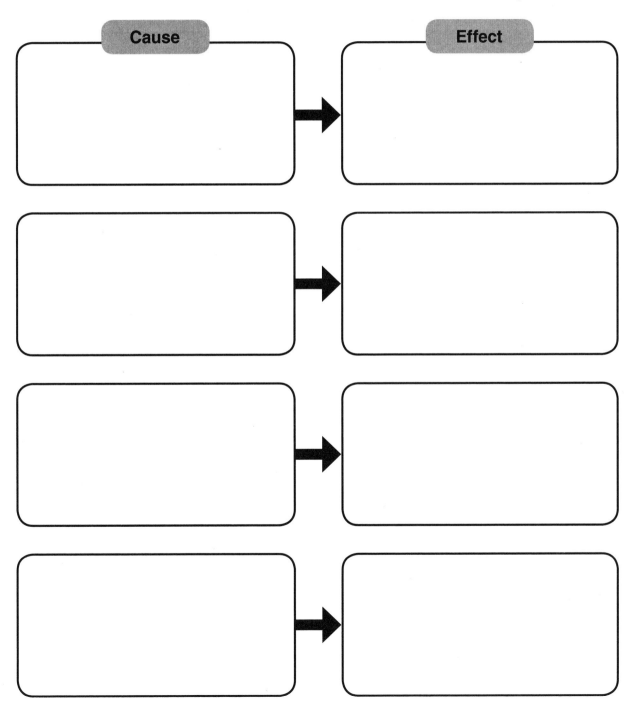

UNIT
2

Cause and Effect

Write a cause-and-effect essay about **how using insects as a food source instead of beef cattle could be beneficial.**

• Explain how growing and eating insects could affect humans and Earth's atmosphere.

_____

Title

_____

_____

_____

_____

_____

_____

_____

_____

_____

_____

_____

_____

Name _____

Evaluate Your Writing

Read about the cause-and-effect text structure. Then use your essay to complete the activity below.

> A text that has a **cause-and-effect** structure tells what happens (effect) and why it happens (cause). It also tells if a cause has multiple effects.

The reason for writing is clear.

My essay described the cause-and-effect relationship(s) between: _____

_____

I used these cause-and-effect signal words:

_____   _____   _____

I provided details that support the topic.

I included these detail sentences:

    1. _____

    2. _____

My paragraphs have a clear focus.

My first paragraph explains that _____

caused (or causes) _____

My last paragraph summarizes the cause-and-effect relationship(s) with this sentence:

_____

Building a Better Nest

Lesson Objectives

Writing
Students use information from the science article to write an explanatory essay.

Vocabulary
Students learn content vocabulary words and use those words to write about how birds are similar to engineers and architects.

Content Knowledge
Students learn how and why birds and professionals build structures that are safe, attractive, and sturdy.

Essential Understanding
Students understand that birds have many of the same building standards as engineers and architects.

Prepare the Unit

Reproduce and distribute one copy for each student.

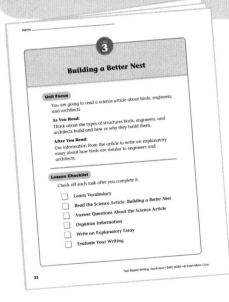

1 **Unit Focus and Lesson Checklist**

Distribute one unit to each student and direct students' attention to the Unit Focus and Lesson Checklist. Tell them they will be able to refer to the focus of the unit as needed while working on the lessons. Instruct students to check off each task on the checklist after they complete it.

Read aloud the focus statements, and verify that students understand their purpose for reading. Ask:

• *What are we going to read about?* (birds, engineers, and architects)

• *What are you going to learn about them?* (how and why they build the types of structures that they do)

• *What are you going to write based on this article?* (an explanatory essay)

CCSS: **W** 5.2, 5.4, 5.8   **RIT** 5.3, 5.4, 5.10

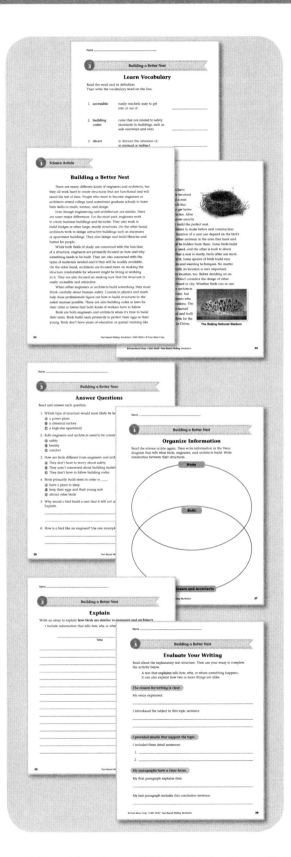

2 Learn Vocabulary

Read aloud each content vocabulary word and have students repeat. Then read aloud and discuss the definitions. Explain that students will have a better understanding of the words after they read the science article. Have students write the vocabulary words on the provided lines.

3 Read the Science Article: *Building a Better Nest*

Read aloud the science article as students follow along silently. Then have students reread the article independently or in small groups.

4 Answer Questions About the Science Article

To ensure reading comprehension, have students answer the text-dependent questions. Review the answers together.

5 Organize Information

Explain to students that they will use a Venn diagram to help them plan their essays. Guide students in using the text to complete the organizer.

6 Write an Explanatory Essay

Have students complete the writing assignment independently, with a partner, or in small groups.

Review the structure of an explanatory essay:

- Tells how, why, or where something happens
- Explains how two or more things are similar
- Includes an introductory topic sentence and a conclusion sentence at the end

7 Evaluate Your Writing

Explain that students will evaluate their writing to ensure that they have produced well-written essays that follow the explanatory text structure.

UNIT
3

Building a Better Nest

Unit Focus

You are going to read a science article about birds, engineers, and architects.

As You Read:

Think about the types of structures birds, engineers, and architects build and how or why they build them.

After You Read:

Use information from the article to write an explanatory essay about how birds are similar to engineers and architects.

Lesson Checklist

Check off each task after you complete it.

- [ ] Learn Vocabulary
- [ ] Read the Science Article: *Building a Better Nest*
- [ ] Answer Questions About the Science Article
- [ ] Organize Information
- [ ] Write an Explanatory Essay
- [ ] Evaluate Your Writing

Learn Vocabulary

Read the word and its definition.
Then write the vocabulary word on the line.

1. **accessible**   easily reached; easy to get into or out of   _____

2. **building codes**   rules that are related to safety standards in buildings, such as safe stairways and exits   _____

3. **divert**   to distract the attention of; to mislead or redirect   _____

4. **functional**   able to work properly and productively   _____

5. **graduate schools**   schools where students can earn master's or doctorate degrees   _____

6. **hone**   to improve or perfect   _____

7. **instinct**   a behavior that a person or an animal is born with; a behavior that comes naturally   _____

8. **weaving**   wrapping threads or other materials together   _____

Building a Better Nest

There are many different kinds of engineers and architects, but they all work hard to create structures that are functional and will stand the test of time. People who want to become engineers or architects attend college (and sometimes graduate school) to hone their skills in math, science, and design.

Even though engineering and architecture are similar, there are some major differences. For the most part, engineers work to create business buildings and factories. They also work to build bridges or other large, sturdy structures. On the other hand, architects work to design attractive buildings such as museums or apartment buildings. They also design and build libraries and homes for people.

While both fields of study are concerned with the function of a structure, engineers are primarily focused on how and why something needs to be built. They are also concerned with the types of materials needed and if they will be readily available. On the other hand, architects are focused more on making the structure comfortable for whoever might be living or working in it. They are also focused on making sure that the structure is easily accessible and attractive.

When either engineers or architects build something, they must think carefully about human safety. Courses in physics and math help these professionals figure out how to build structures in the safest manner possible. There are also building codes or laws for their cities or towns that both kinds of workers have to follow.

Birds are both engineers and architects when it's time to build their nests. Birds build nests primarily to protect their eggs or their young. Birds don't have years of education or special training like

humans do, but scientists have learned that there is more involved in a bird's ability to build a nest than just instinct. Research has shown that birds actually get better at building nests with practice. After many years, a bird will know exactly how, when, and where to build the perfect nest.

A bird has many decisions to make before nest construction begins. For example, the location of a nest can depend on the bird's predators. There may be other animals in the area that hunt and kill birds, so the nest must be hidden from them. Some birds build two nests. One is actually used, and the other is built to divert predators. To make sure that a nest is sturdy, birds often use more than one material to build it. Some species of birds build very complex nests, using knots and weaving techniques. No matter what type of nest birds build, its location is very important.

An architect considers location, too. Before deciding on an architectural style, an architect considers the design of other buildings in the neighborhood or city. Whether birds can or can not be called engineers or architects might be a matter of opinion, but there was a team of architects who were inspired by their creations. The Beijing National Stadium named "Bird's Nest" was designed and built by a Swiss architectural firm for the 2008 Summer Olympics in China.

The Beijing National Stadium

Building a Better Nest

Answer Questions

Read and answer each question.

1. Which type of structure would most likely be built by an architect?

Ⓐ a power plant

Ⓑ a chemical factory

Ⓒ a high-rise apartment

2. Both engineers and architects need to be concerned about ____.

Ⓐ safety

Ⓑ beauty

Ⓒ comfort

3. How are birds different from engineers and architects?

Ⓐ They don't have to worry about safety.

Ⓑ They aren't concerned about building materials.

Ⓒ They don't have to follow building codes.

4. Birds primarily build nests in order to ____.

Ⓐ have a place to sleep

Ⓑ keep their eggs and their young safe

Ⓒ attract other birds

5. Why would a bird build a nest that it will not use because of predators? Explain.

_____

_____

6. How is a bird like an engineer? Use one example from the article.

_____

_____

Organize Information

Read the science article again. Then write information in the Venn diagram that tells what birds, engineers, and architects build. Write similarities between their structures.

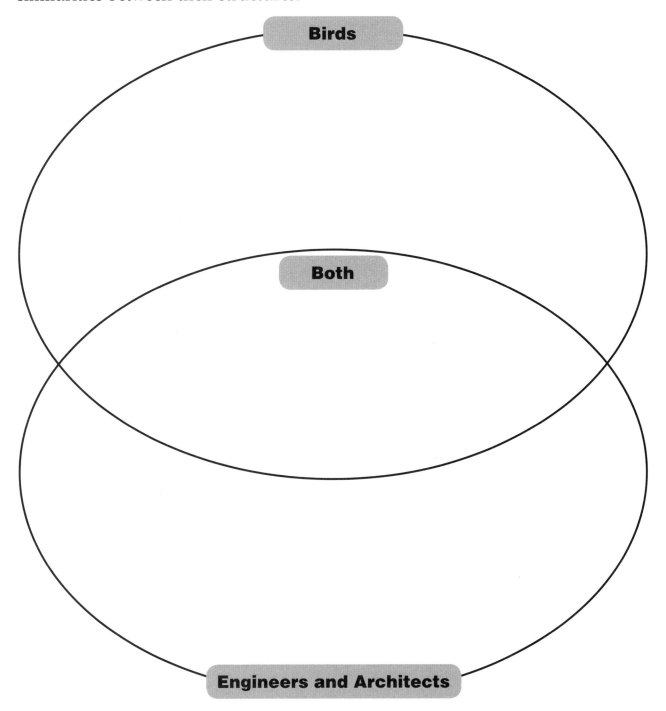

Birds

Both

Engineers and Architects

Name _____

Building a Better Nest

Explain

Write an essay to explain **how birds are similar to engineers and architects.**

• Include information that tells *how, why,* or *where.*

_____
Title

_____

_____

_____

_____

_____

_____

_____

_____

_____

_____

_____

_____

_____

_____

Name _____

Evaluate Your Writing

Read about the explanatory text structure. Then use your essay to complete the activity below.

> A text that **explains** tells how, why, or where something happens. It can also explain how two or more things are alike.

The reason for writing is clear.

My essay explained:

_____

I introduced the subject in this topic sentence:

_____

_____

I provided details that support the topic.

I included these detail sentences:

1. _____

2. _____

My paragraphs have a clear focus.

My first paragraph explains that:

_____

My last paragraph includes this conclusion sentence:

_____

Fabulous Foods

Lesson Objectives

Writing
Students use information from the health article to write an explanatory essay.

Vocabulary
Students learn content vocabulary words and use those words to write about why they should grow their own produce.

Content Knowledge
Students learn about the MyPlate program and how to grow their own gardens.

Essential Understanding
Students understand that growing their own fruits and vegetables can be beneficial to both their health and their budgets.

Prepare the Unit

Reproduce and distribute one copy for each student.

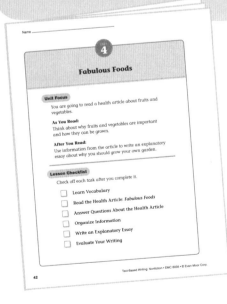

1 Unit Focus and Lesson Checklist

Distribute one unit to each student and direct students' attention to the Unit Focus and Lesson Checklist. Tell them they will be able to refer to the focus of the unit as needed while working on the lessons. Instruct students to check off each task on the checklist after they complete it.

Read aloud the focus statements, and verify that students understand their purpose for reading. Ask:

- *What are we going to read about?* (fruits and vegetables)

- *What are you going to learn about them?* (their importance and how they are grown)

- *What are you going to write based on this article?* (an explanatory essay)

CCSS: **W** 5.2, 5.4, 5.8   **RIT** 5.3, 5.4, 5.10

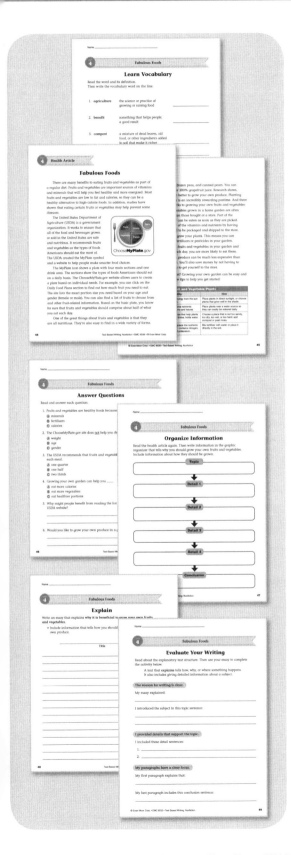

2 **Learn Vocabulary**

Read aloud each content vocabulary word and have students repeat. Then read aloud and discuss the definitions. Explain that students will have a better understanding of the words after they read the health article. Have students write the vocabulary words on the provided lines.

3 **Read the Health Article:** *Fabulous Foods*

Read aloud the health article as students follow along silently. Then have students reread the article independently or in small groups.

4 **Answer Questions About the Health Article**

To ensure reading comprehension, have students answer the text-dependent questions. Review the answers together.

5 **Organize Information**

Explain to students that they will use a topic-and-details graphic organizer to help them plan their essays. Guide students in using the text to complete the organizer.

6 **Write an Explanatory Essay**

Have students complete the writing assignment independently, with a partner, or in small groups.

Review the structure of an explanatory essay:

- Tells how, why, or where something happens
- Includes specific details about the topic
- Includes an introductory topic sentence and a conclusion sentence at the end

7 **Evaluate Your Writing**

Explain that students will evaluate their writing to ensure that they have produced well-written essays that follow the explanatory text structure.

UNIT
4

Fabulous Foods

Unit Focus

You are going to read a health article about fruits and vegetables.

As You Read:

Think about why fruits and vegetables are important and how they can be grown.

After You Read:

Use information from the article to write an explanatory essay about why you should grow your own garden.

Lesson Checklist

Check off each task after you complete it.

- [ ] **Learn Vocabulary**
- [ ] **Read the Health Article: _Fabulous Foods_**
- [ ] **Answer Questions About the Health Article**
- [ ] **Organize Information**
- [ ] **Write an Explanatory Essay**
- [ ] **Evaluate Your Writing**

Name _____

Learn Vocabulary

Read the word and its definition.
Then write the vocabulary word on the line.

1. **agriculture**   the science or practice of
                       growing or raising food   _____

2. **benefit**   something that helps people;
                       a good result   _____

3. **compost**   a mixture of dead leaves, old
                       food, or other ingredients added
                       to soil that make it richer   _____

4. **comprise**   to include or be made up of   _____

5. **fertilizers**   substances that help plants grow
                       larger or more quickly   _____

6. **pesticides**   chemicals that are used on
                       plants or fields to kill insects   _____

7. **portion**   amount or size   _____

8. **produce**   fruits and vegetables   _____

9. **tending**   caring for or raising   _____

Fabulous Foods

There are many benefits to eating fruits and vegetables as part of a regular diet. Fruits and vegetables are important sources of vitamins and minerals that will help you feel healthy and more energized. Most fruits and vegetables are low in fat and calories, so they can be a healthy alternative to high-calorie foods. In addition, studies have shown that eating certain fruits or vegetables may help prevent some diseases.

The United States Department of Agriculture (USDA) is a government organization. It works to ensure that all of the food and beverages grown or sold in the United States are safe and nutritious. It recommends fruits and vegetables as the types of foods Americans should eat the most of. The USDA created the MyPlate symbol and a website to help people make smarter food choices.

The MyPlate icon shows a plate with four main sections and one drink area. The sections show the types of foods Americans should eat on a daily basis. The ChooseMyPlate.gov website allows users to create a plate based on individual needs. For example, you can click on the Daily Food Plans section to find out how much fruit you need to eat. The site lists the exact portion size you need based on your age and gender (female or male). You can also find a list of fruits to choose from and other fruit-related information. Based on the basic plate, you know for sure that fruits and vegetables should comprise about half of what you eat each day.

One of the great things about fruits and vegetables is that they are all nutritious. They're also easy to find in a wide variety of forms.

You can find fresh corn, frozen peas, and canned pears. You can also find dried apricots or 100% grapefruit juice. Research shows, however, that it might be better to grow your own produce. Planting and harvesting a garden is an incredibly rewarding pastime. And there are additional health perks to growing your own fruits and vegetables:

- The fruits and vegetables grown in a home garden are often more nutritious than those bought at a store. Part of the reason is that they can be eaten as soon as they are picked. You won't lose any of the vitamins and nutrients by having to wait for the food to be packaged and shipped to the store.

- You decide how to grow your plants. This means you can control the use of fertilizers or pesticides in your garden.

- If you are growing fruits and vegetables in your garden and tending to them each day, you are more likely to eat them.

- Growing your own produce can be much less expensive than buying it at a store. You'll also save money by not having to put gas in your car to get yourself to the store.

Are you convinced yet? Growing your own garden can be easy and rewarding. Here are a few tips to help you get started:

Fruit and Vegetable Plants		
Need	**Why**	**How**
Sunshine	Plants use the energy from the sun as a food source.	Place plants in direct sunlight, or choose plants that grow well in the shade.
Water	It helps plants move nutrients through their stems and leaves.	Place plants near a water source so they can easily be watered daily.
Good soil	It contains minerals that help plants stay healthy and thrive; holds water.	Choose a place that is not too sandy, too dry, too wet, or too hard; add compost or peat moss.
Fertilizer	It helps plants replace the nutrients they use to grow; contains nitrogen, phosphorus, and potassium.	Mix fertilizer with water or place it directly in the soil.

Name _____

Answer Questions

Read and answer each question.

1. Fruits and vegetables are healthy foods because they are low in ___.

    Ⓐ minerals

    Ⓑ fertilizers

    Ⓒ calories

2. The ChooseMyPlate.gov site does <u>not</u> help you choose foods based on your ___.

    Ⓐ weight

    Ⓑ age

    Ⓒ gender

3. The USDA recommends that fruits and vegetables make up about ___ of each meal.

    Ⓐ one quarter

    Ⓑ one half

    Ⓒ two thirds

4. Growing your own garden can help you ___.

    Ⓐ eat more calories

    Ⓑ eat more vegetables

    Ⓒ eat healthier portions

5. Why might people benefit from reading the list of vegetables on the USDA website?

    _____

    _____

6. Would you like to grow your own produce in a garden? Why or why not?

    _____

    _____

Name _____

Organize Information

Read the health article again. Then write information in the graphic organizer that tells why you should grow your own fruits and vegetables. Include information about how they should be grown.

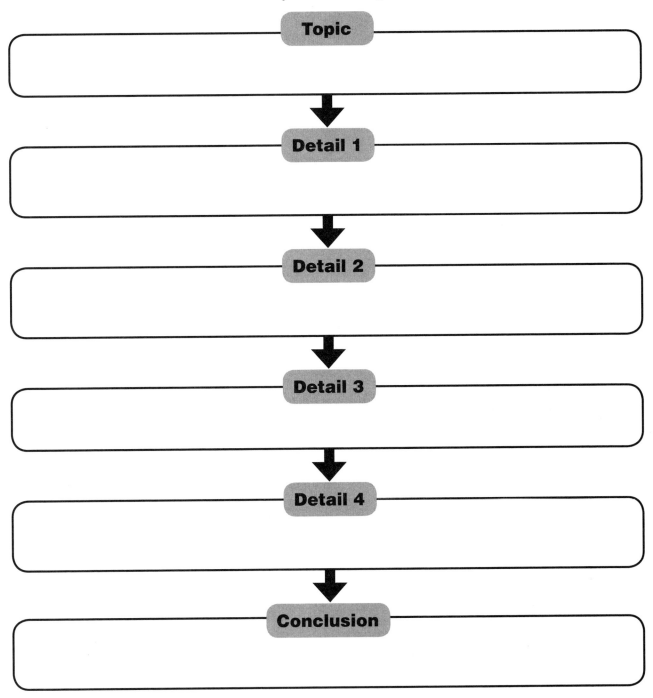

Topic

Detail 1

Detail 2

Detail 3

Detail 4

Conclusion

Name _____

Explain

Write an essay that explains **why it is beneficial to grow your own fruits and vegetables**.

- Include information that tells how you should grow your own produce.

_____

Title

_____

_____

_____

_____

_____

_____

_____

_____

_____

_____

_____

_____

Name _____

Evaluate Your Writing

Read about the explanatory text structure. Then use your essay to complete the activity below.

A text that **explains** tells how, why, or where something happens. It also includes giving detailed information about a subject.

The reason for writing is clear.

My essay explained:

_____

I introduced the subject in this topic sentence:

_____

_____

I provided details that support the topic.

I included these detail sentences:

1. _____

2. _____

My paragraphs have a clear focus.

My first paragraph explains that:

_____

My last paragraph includes this conclusion sentence:

_____

Sonia Sotomayor

Lesson Objectives

Writing
Students use information from the biography to write a sequence essay.

Vocabulary
Students learn content vocabulary words and use those words to write about the major events in Sonia Sotomayor's lifetime.

Content Knowledge
Students learn about Sotomayor's difficult childhood and her education and successes.

Essential Understanding
Students understand that people can overcome obstacles and go on to be very successful through education.

Prepare the Unit

Reproduce and distribute one copy for each student.

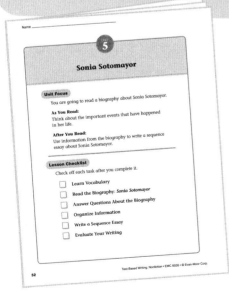

1 Unit Focus and Lesson Checklist

Distribute one unit to each student and direct students' attention to the Unit Focus and Lesson Checklist. Tell them they will be able to refer to the focus of the unit as needed while working on the lessons. Instruct students to check off each task on the checklist after they complete it.

Read aloud the focus statements, and verify that students understand their purpose for reading. Ask:

• *Who are we going to read about?* (Sonia Sotomayor)

• *What are you going to learn about her?* (the important events in her lifetime)

• *What are you going to write based on this biography?* (a sequence essay)

CCSS: **W** 5.2, 5.4, 5.8 **RIT** 5.3, 5.4, 5.10

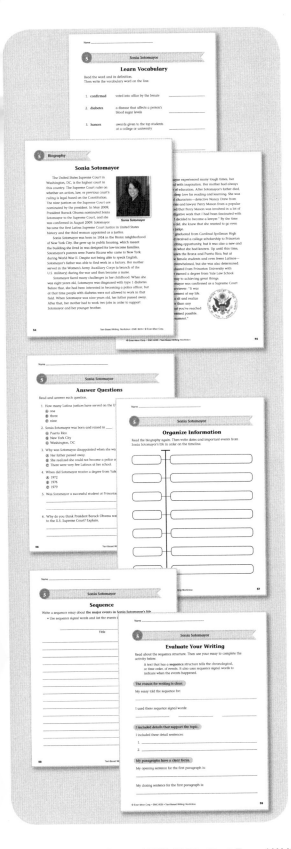

2 Learn Vocabulary

Read aloud each content vocabulary word and have students repeat. Then read aloud and discuss the definitions. Explain that students will have a better understanding of the words after they read the biography. Have students write the vocabulary words on the provided lines.

3 Read the Biography: *Sonia Sotomayor*

Read aloud the biography as students follow along silently. Then have students reread the biography independently or in small groups.

4 Answer Questions About the Biography

To ensure reading comprehension, have students answer the text-dependent questions. Review the answers together.

5 Organize Information

Explain to students that they will use a timeline graphic organizer to help them plan their essays. Guide students in using the text to complete the organizer.

6 Write a Sequence Essay

Have students complete the writing assignment independently, with a partner, or in small groups.

Review the structure of a sequence essay and the related signal words:

- Tells the chronological order, or time order, of events

- Allows readers to understand exactly when events happened

- Signal words: *before, during, after, when, then, earlier, later, while, first, next*

7 Evaluate Your Writing

Explain that students will evaluate their writing to ensure that they have produced well-written essays that follow the sequence text structure.

UNIT
5

Sonia Sotomayor

Unit Focus

You are going to read a biography about Sonia Sotomayor.

As You Read:

Think about the important events that have happened in her life.

After You Read:

Use information from the biography to write a sequence essay about Sonia Sotomayor.

Lesson Checklist

Check off each task after you complete it.

- [ ] **Learn Vocabulary**
- [ ] **Read the Biography:** *Sonia Sotomayor*
- [ ] **Answer Questions About the Biography**
- [ ] **Organize Information**
- [ ] **Write a Sequence Essay**
- [ ] **Evaluate Your Writing**

Learn Vocabulary

Read the word and its definition.
Then write the vocabulary word on the line.

1. **confirmed**   voted into office by the Senate   _____

2. **diabetes**   a disease that affects a person's
blood sugar levels   _____

3. **honors**   awards given to the top students
at a college or university   _____

4. **justices**   judges; people who decide on the
fairness or unfairness of an action
in a court of law   _____

5. **legal**   in agreement with the law   _____

6. **nominated**   chosen to have a specific job or
to run for a specific office   _____

7. **rules**   decides; makes judgments   _____

8. **scholarship**   free money given to a student
to help pay for schooling   _____

Sonia Sotomayor

The United States Supreme Court in Washington, DC, is the highest court in this country. The Supreme Court rules on whether an action, law, or previous court's ruling is legal based on the Constitution. The nine justices on the Supreme Court are nominated by the president. In May 2009, President Barack Obama nominated Sonia Sotomayor to the Supreme Court, and she was confirmed in August 2009. Sotomayor

Sonia Sotomayor

became the first Latina Supreme Court Justice in United States history and the third woman appointed as a justice.

Sonia Sotomayor was born in 1954 in the Bronx neighborhood of New York City. She grew up in public housing, which meant the building she lived in was designed for low-income families. Sotomayor's parents were Puerto Ricans who came to New York during World War II. Despite not being able to speak English, Sotomayor's father was able to find work in a factory. Her mother served in the Women's Army Auxiliary Corps (a branch of the U.S. military) during the war and then became a nurse.

Sotomayor faced many challenges in her childhood. When she was eight years old, Sotomayor was diagnosed with type 1 diabetes. Before that, she had been interested in becoming a police officer, but at that time people with diabetes were not allowed to work in that field. When Sotomayor was nine years old, her father passed away. After that, her mother had to work two jobs in order to support Sotomayor and her younger brother.

Text-Based Writing: Nonfiction • EMC 6035 • © Evan-Moor Corp.

Even though Sotomayor experienced many tough times, her childhood was also filled with inspiration. Her mother had always stressed the importance of education. After Sotomayor's father died, Sotomayor developed a deep love for reading and learning. She was inspired by two fictional characters—detective Nancy Drew from the *Nancy Drew* book series and lawyer Perry Mason from a popular television show. "I noticed that Perry Mason was involved in a lot of the same kinds of investigative work that I had been fascinated with reading *Nancy Drew,* so I decided to become a lawyer." By the time Sotomayor was 10 years old, she knew that she wanted to go even further—and become a judge.

In 1972, Sotomayor graduated from Cardinal Spellman High School in the Bronx and received a college scholarship to Princeton University. It was an exciting opportunity, but it was also a new and very different world from what she had known. Up until this time, Sotomayor had only known the Bronx and Puerto Rico, but at Princeton there were few female students and even fewer Latinos— only about 20. She felt overwhelmed, but she was also determined. In 1976, Sotomayor graduated from Princeton University with top honors. In 1979, she earned a degree from Yale Law School. Sotomayor was on her way to achieving great things.

In 2009, when Sotomayor was confirmed as a Supreme Court Justice, she told one interviewer: "It was the most electrifying moment of my life. A moment in which you sit and realize that you've gone further than any dream you ever had, that you've reached something that never seemed possible. It is an overwhelming moment."

Name _____

Answer Questions

Read and answer each question.

1. How many Latina justices have served on the U.S. Supreme Court?
   - Ⓐ one
   - Ⓑ three
   - Ⓒ nine

2. Sonia Sotomayor was born and raised in ___.
   - Ⓐ Puerto Rico
   - Ⓑ New York City
   - Ⓒ Washington, DC

3. Why was Sotomayor disappointed when she was eight years old?
   - Ⓐ Her father passed away.
   - Ⓑ She realized she could not become a police officer.
   - Ⓒ There were very few Latinos at her school.

4. When did Sotomayor receive a degree from Yale Law School?
   - Ⓐ 1972
   - Ⓑ 1976
   - Ⓒ 1979

5. Was Sotomayor a successful student at Princeton? How do you know?

   _____

   _____

6. Why do you think President Barack Obama nominated Sotomayor
   to the U.S. Supreme Court? Explain.

   _____

   _____

Organize Information

Read the biography again. Then write dates and important events from Sonia Sotomayor's life in order on the timeline.

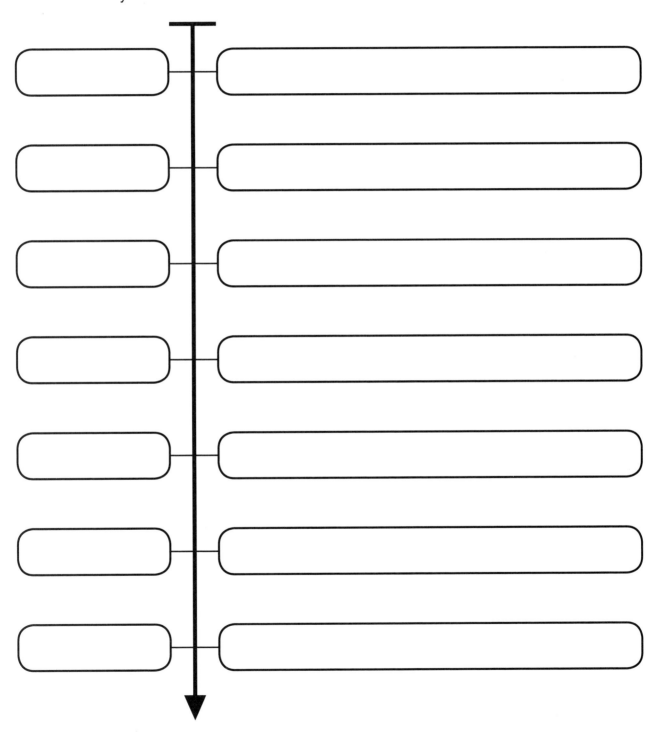

UNIT 5

Sequence

Write a sequence essay about **the major events in Sonia Sotomayor's life**.

- Use sequence signal words and list the events in order.

_____
Title

_____

_____

_____

_____

_____

_____

_____

_____

_____

_____

_____

_____

_____

_____

Sonia Sotomayor

Evaluate Your Writing

Read about the sequence structure. Then use your essay to complete the activity below.

> A text that has a **sequence** structure tells the chronological, or time order, of events. It also uses sequence signal words to indicate when the events happened.

The reason for writing is clear.

My essay told the sequence for:

_____

I used these sequence signal words:

_____   _____   _____

I included details that support the topic.

I included these detail sentences:

1. _____

2. _____

My paragraphs have a clear focus.

My opening sentence for the first paragraph is:

_____

My closing sentence for the first paragraph is:

_____

Transportation Over Time

Lesson Objectives

Writing
Students use information from the social studies article to write a compare-and-contrast essay.

Vocabulary
Students learn content vocabulary words and use those words to compare and contrast modes of transportation throughout history.

Content Knowledge
Students learn the designs and functions of the basic wheel, the bicycle, and the car.

Essential Understanding
Students understand that transportation has come a long way, but it could still change dramatically in the future.

Prepare the Unit

Reproduce and distribute one copy for each student.

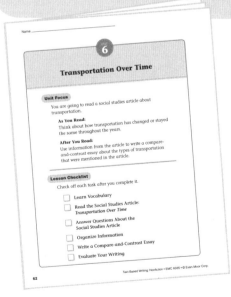

1 Unit Focus and Lesson Checklist

Distribute one unit to each student and direct students' attention to the Unit Focus and Lesson Checklist. Tell them they will be able to refer to the focus of the unit as needed while working on the lessons. Instruct students to check off each task on the checklist after they complete it.

Read aloud the focus statements, and verify that students understand their purpose for reading. Ask:

- *What are we going to read about?* (transportation)

- *What are you going to learn about it?* (how it has changed or stayed the same)

- *What are you going to write based on this article?* (a compare-and-contrast essay)

CCSS: W 5.2, 5.4, 5.8   RIT 5.3, 5.4, 5.10

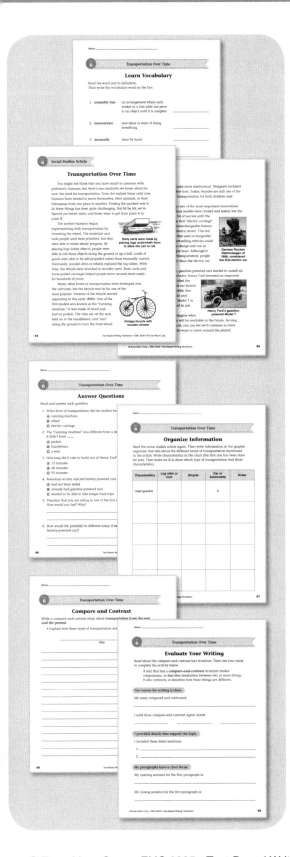

2 Learn Vocabulary

Read aloud each content vocabulary word and have students repeat. Then read aloud and discuss the definitions. Explain that students will have a better understanding of the words after they read the social studies article. Have students write the vocabulary words on the provided lines.

3 Read the Social Studies Article: *Transportation Over Time*

Read aloud the social studies article as students follow along silently. Then have students reread the article independently or in small groups.

4 Answer Questions About the Social Studies Article

To ensure reading comprehension, have students answer the text-dependent questions. Review the answers together.

5 Organize Information

Explain to students that they will use a compare-and-contrast graphic organizer to help them plan their essays. Guide students in using the text to complete the organizer.

6 Write a Compare-and-Contrast Essay

Have students complete the writing assignment independently, with a partner, or in small groups.

Review the structure of a compare-and-contrast essay and the related signal words:

- Explains similarities and differences between two or more things

- Signal words: *same, alike, also, as well, both; different, however, but, while, instead of*

7 Evaluate Your Writing

Explain that students will evaluate their writing to ensure that they have produced well-written essays that follow the compare-and-contrast text structure.

UNIT
6

Transportation Over Time

Unit Focus

You are going to read a social studies article about transportation.

As You Read:

Think about how transportation has changed or stayed the same throughout the years.

After You Read:

Use information from the article to write a compare-and-contrast essay about the types of transportation that were mentioned in the article.

Lesson Checklist

Check off each task after you complete it.

☐ **Learn Vocabulary**

☐ **Read the Social Studies Article:**
Transportation Over Time

☐ **Answer Questions About the**
Social Studies Article

☐ **Organize Information**

☐ **Write a Compare-and-Contrast Essay**

☐ **Evaluate Your Writing**

Learn Vocabulary

Read the word and its definition.
Then write the vocabulary word on the line.

1. **assembly line**   an arrangement where each worker in a line adds one piece to an object until it is complete   _____

2. **innovations**   new ideas or ways of doing something   _____

3. **manually**   done by hand   _____

4. **mechanical**   including or using machine parts   _____

5. **primitive**   relating to the earliest form of something   _____

6. **rechargeable**   able to hold an electric charge multiple times and still work   _____

7. **self-propelled**   able to move under its own weight or power   _____

Transportation Over Time

You might not think that you have much in common with prehistoric humans, but there's one similarity we know about for sure: the need for transportation. From the earliest times until now, humans have needed to move themselves, their animals, or their belongings from one place to another. Finding the quickest way to do these things has been quite challenging. But bit by bit, we've figured out better, safer, and faster ways to get from point A to point B.

The earliest humans began experimenting with transportation by inventing the wheel. The materials and tools people used were primitive, but they were able to make steady progress. By placing logs under objects, people were

Early carts were made by placing logs underneath them to allow the cart to roll.

able to roll those objects along the ground or up a hill. Loads of goods were able to be self-propelled rather than manually carried. Eventually, wooden discs or wheels replaced the log rollers. With time, the wheels were attached to wooden carts. Basic carts and horse-pulled carriages helped people move around more easily for hundreds of years.

Many other forms of transportation were developed over the centuries, but the bicycle was by far one of the most popular. Versions of the bicycle started appearing in the early 1800s. One of the first models was known as the "running machine." It was made of wood and had no pedals. The rider sat on the seat, held on to the handlebars, and "ran" along the ground to turn the front wheel.

Vintage bicycle with wooden wheels

Over time, bicycles became more mechanical. Designers included pedals, gears, and rubber tires. Today, bicycles are still one of the most popular forms of transportation for both children and adults.

The automobile was one of the most important innovations in transportation. Various models were created and tested, but the industry didn't have a lot of success until the 1830s. At that time, the first "electric carriage" was created. It had a nonrechargeable battery that powered a small electric motor. This led to the creation of cars that used rechargeable batteries. One of the best-selling vehicles could go 40 miles on a single charge and run at speeds up to 15 miles per hour. Although it was a "clean" form of transportation, people wanted to travel farther than the electric car batteries would allow.

German Flocken Elektrowagen of 1888, considered the first electric car

By the early 1900s, gasoline-powered cars started to outsell all other types of motor vehicles. Henry Ford invented an improved assembly line and installed the first conveyor belt in his car factory around 1913. The assembly line lowered production costs and allowed Ford's famous Model T to be completely assembled in just 93 minutes.

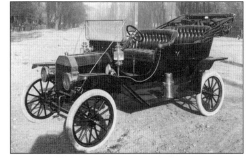

Henry Ford's gasoline-powered Model T

It's interesting to imagine what kinds of transportation will be available in the future. As long as humans need to travel, you can bet we'll continue to strive for even better and faster ways to move around the planet!

Answer Questions

Read and answer each question.

1. What form of transportation did the earliest humans experiment with?
   - Ⓐ running machine
   - Ⓑ wheel
   - Ⓒ electric carriage

2. The "running machine" was different from a modern bicycle because it didn't have ___.
   - Ⓐ pedals
   - Ⓑ handlebars
   - Ⓒ a seat

3. How long did it take to build one of Henry Ford's Model T cars?
   - Ⓐ 15 minutes
   - Ⓑ 40 minutes
   - Ⓒ 93 minutes

4. American society rejected battery-powered cars because they ___.
   - Ⓐ had not been tested
   - Ⓑ already had gasoline-powered cars
   - Ⓒ wanted to be able to take longer road trips

5. Visualize that you are riding in one of the first gasoline-powered cars. How would you feel? Why?

   _____

   _____

6. How would life probably be different today if we had kept using battery-powered cars?

   _____

   _____

Name _____

Organize Information

Read the social studies article again. Then write information in the graphic organizer that tells about the different forms of transportation mentioned in the article. Write characteristics in the chart (the first one has been done for you). Then make an **X** to show which type of transportation had those characteristics.

Characteristics	Log roller or Cart	Bicycle	Car or Automobile	Notes
Used gasoline			X	

Name _____

Compare and Contrast

Write a compare-and-contrast essay about **transportation from the past and the present**.

- Explain how these types of transportation are alike and different.

_____
Title

_____

_____

_____

_____

_____

_____

_____

_____

_____

_____

_____

_____

Name _____

Evaluate Your Writing

Read about the compare-and-contrast text structure. Then use your essay to complete the activity below.

> A text that has a **compare-and-contrast** structure makes comparisons, or describes similarities between two or more things. It also contrasts, or describes how these things are different.

The reason for writing is clear.

My essay compared and contrasted:

_____

I used these compare-and-contrast signal words:

_____   _____   _____

I provided details that support the topic.

I included these detail sentences:

1. _____

2. _____

My paragraphs have a clear focus.

My opening sentence for the first paragraph is:

_____

My closing sentence for the first paragraph is:

_____

Paula Hammond

Lesson Objectives

Writing
Students use information from the biography to write an opinion essay.

Vocabulary
Students learn content vocabulary words and use those words to write about Paula Hammond's achievements.

Content Knowledge
Students learn about Paula Hammond's life, family, schooling, and career.

Essential Understanding
Students understand that Paula Hammond was encouraged by her parents and teachers and inspired by her coworkers and colleagues.

Prepare the Unit

Reproduce and distribute one copy for each student.

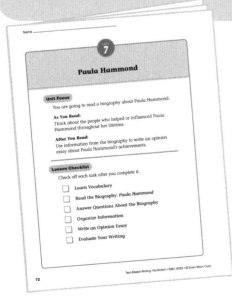

1 Unit Focus and Lesson Checklist

Distribute one unit to each student and direct students' attention to the Unit Focus and Lesson Checklist. Tell them they will be able to refer to the focus of the unit as needed while working on the lessons. Instruct students to check off each task on the checklist after they complete it.

Read aloud the focus statements, and verify that students understand their purpose for reading. Ask:

• *Who are we going to read about?* (Paula Hammond)

• *What are you going to learn about her?* (how people helped or influenced her)

• *What are you going to write based on this article?* (an opinion essay)

CCSS: **W** 5.1, 5.4, 5.8   **RIT** 5.3, 5.4, 5.10

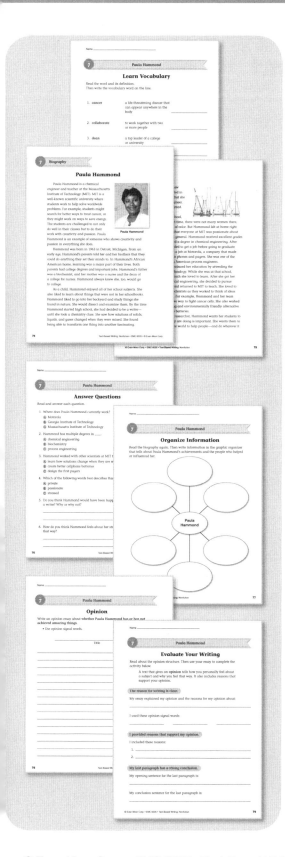

2   Learn Vocabulary

Read aloud each content vocabulary word and have students repeat. Then read aloud and discuss the definitions. Explain that students will have a better understanding of the words after they read the biography. Have students write the vocabulary words on the provided lines.

3   Read the Biography: *Paula Hammond*

Read aloud the biography as students follow along silently. Then have students reread the biography independently or in small groups.

4   Answer Questions About the Biography

To ensure reading comprehension, have students answer the text-dependent questions. Review the answers together.

5   Organize Information

Explain to students that they will use an idea-web graphic organizer to help them plan their essays. Guide students in using the text to complete the organizer.

6   Write an Opinion Essay

Have students complete the writing assignment independently, with a partner, or in small groups.

Remind students that an opinion essay:

- tells how you feel about something,

- tells why you feel that way, and

- includes signal words: *I feel, I think, to me, I like, I agree that; I don't like, I disagree that.*

7   Evaluate Your Writing

Explain that students will evaluate their writing to ensure that they have produced well-written essays that follow the opinion structure.

UNIT
7

Paula Hammond

Unit Focus

You are going to read a biography about Paula Hammond.

As You Read:

Think about the people who helped or influenced Paula Hammond throughout her lifetime.

After You Read:

Use information from the biography to write an opinion essay about Paula Hammond's achievements.

Lesson Checklist

Check off each task after you complete it.

- [ ] **Learn Vocabulary**
- [ ] **Read the Biography:** *Paula Hammond*
- [ ] **Answer Questions About the Biography**
- [ ] **Organize Information**
- [ ] **Write an Opinion Essay**
- [ ] **Evaluate Your Writing**

Name _____

Learn Vocabulary

Read the word and its definition.
Then write the vocabulary word on the line.

1. **cancer**   a life-threatening disease that
                         can appear anywhere in the
                         body   _____

2. **collaborate**   to work together with two
                         or more people   _____

3. **dean**   a top leader of a college
                         or university   _____

4. **dissect**   to take apart piece by piece   _____

5. **environmentally**   safe or healthy; not toxic for
   friendly   the environment, people,
                         or animals   _____

6. **graduate school**   a school that offers advanced
                         programs beyond a college
                         bachelor's degree   _____

7. **pagers**   electronic devices that notify
                         a user if he or she has a
                         message   _____

8. **transform**   to change; to make
                         different   _____

Paula Hammond

Paula Hammond is a chemical engineer and teacher at the Massachusetts Institute of Technology (MIT). MIT is a well-known scientific university where students work to help solve worldwide problems. For example, students might search for better ways to treat cancer, or they might work on ways to save energy. The students are challenged to not only do well in their classes but to do their work with creativity and passion. Paula Hammond is an example of someone who shows creativity and passion in everything she does.

Paula Hammond

Hammond was born in 1963 in Detroit, Michigan. From an early age, Hammond's parents told her and her brothers that they could do anything they set their minds to. In Hammond's African American home, learning was a major part of their lives. Both parents had college degrees and important jobs. Hammond's father was a biochemist, and her mother was a nurse and the dean of a college for nurses. Hammond always knew she, too, would go to college.

As a child, Hammond enjoyed all of her school subjects. She also liked to learn about things that were not in her schoolbooks. Hammond liked to go into her backyard and study things she found in nature. She would dissect and examine them. By the time Hammond started high school, she had decided to be a writer— until she took a chemistry class. She saw how solutions of solids, liquids, and gases changed when they were mixed. She found being able to transform one thing into another fascinating.

Hammond's teacher knew that she was very talented in science and suggested that she become a chemical engineer. Hammond's parents agreed.

After Hammond graduated from high school, she went to MIT. At that time, there were not many women there, and even fewer women of color. But Hammond felt at home right away. It seemed to her that everyone at MIT was passionate about science and learning in general. Hammond received excellent grades in chemistry and earned a degree in chemical engineering. After she graduated, she decided to get a job before going to graduate school. Hammond took a job at Motorola, a company that made and sold the first mobile phones and pagers. She was one of the company's first African American process engineers.

Hammond then continued her education by attending the Georgia Institute of Technology. While she was at that school, she remembered how much she loved to learn. After she got her second degree in chemical engineering, she decided to pursue a teaching job. Hammond returned to MIT to teach. She loved to collaborate with other scientists as they worked to think of ideas that would help people. For example, Hammond and her team invented a more effective way to fight cancer cells. She also worked to create a longer-lasting and environmentally friendly alternative to cellphone and laptop batteries.

As a teacher and a researcher, Hammond wants her students to know that the work they are doing is important. She wants them to be able to go out into the world to help people—and do whatever it is that they want to do.

Paula Hammond

Answer Questions

Read and answer each question.

1. Where does Paula Hammond currently work?

    Ⓐ Motorola

    Ⓑ Georgia Institute of Technology

    Ⓒ Massachusetts Institute of Technology

2. Hammond has multiple degrees in ____.

    Ⓐ chemical engineering

    Ⓑ biochemistry

    Ⓒ process engineering

3. Hammond worked with other scientists at MIT to ____.

    Ⓐ learn how solutions change when they are mixed

    Ⓑ create better cellphone batteries

    Ⓒ design the first pagers

4. Which of the following words best describes Hammond?

    Ⓐ private

    Ⓑ passionate

    Ⓒ stressed

5. Do you think Hammond would have been happy if she had become a writer? Why or why not?

    _____

    _____

6. How do you think Hammond feels about her students? Why do you feel that way?

    _____

    _____

Name _____

Organize Information

Read the biography again. Then write information in the graphic organizer that tells about Paula Hammond's achievements and the people who helped or influenced her.

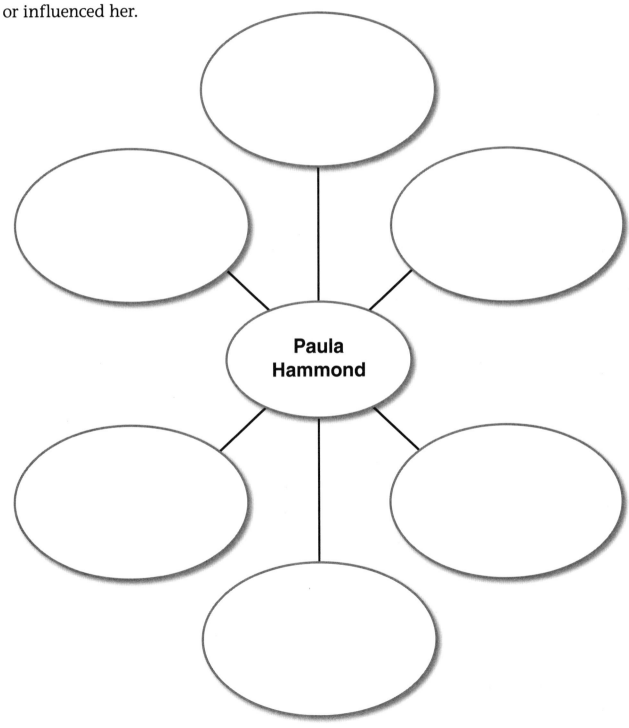

Paula Hammond

UNIT
7

Paula Hammond

Opinion

Write an opinion essay about **whether Paula Hammond has or has not achieved amazing things.**

- Use opinion signal words.

_____
Title

_____

_____

_____

_____

_____

_____

_____

_____

_____

_____

_____

_____

_____

_____

UNIT
7

Evaluate Your Writing

Read about the opinion structure. Then use your essay to complete the activity below.

> A text that gives an **opinion** tells how you personally feel about a subject and why you feel that way. It also includes reasons that support your opinion.

The reason for writing is clear.

My essay explained my opinion and the reasons for my opinion about:

_____

I used these opinion signal words:

_____   _____   _____

I provided reasons that support my opinion.

I included these reasons:

1. _____

2. _____

My last paragraph has a strong conclusion.

My opening sentence for the last paragraph is:

_____

My conclusion sentence for the last paragraph is:

_____

A Matter of Facts

Lesson Objectives

Writing

Students use information from the how-to article to write an opinion essay.

Vocabulary

Students learn content vocabulary words and use those words to write about whether students should or should not be required to fact-check their school reports.

Content Knowledge

Students learn how to find and verify the most accurate and reliable information.

Essential Understanding

Students understand that fact-checking is important for both their current schoolwork and their futures.

Prepare the Unit

Reproduce and distribute one copy for each student.

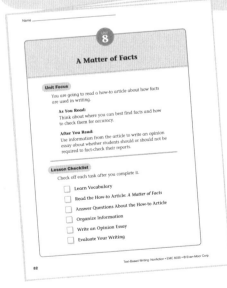

1 Unit Focus and Lesson Checklist

Distribute one unit to each student and direct students' attention to the Unit Focus and Lesson Checklist. Tell them they will be able to refer to the focus of the unit as needed while working on the lessons. Instruct students to check off each task on the checklist after they complete it.

Read aloud the focus statements, and verify that students understand their purpose for reading. Ask:

• *What are we going to read about?* (facts in writing)

• *What are you going to learn about them?* (how to find and check them)

• *What are you going to write based on this article?* (an opinion essay)

CCSS: **W** 5.1, 5.4, 5.8   **RIT** 5.3, 5.4, 5.10

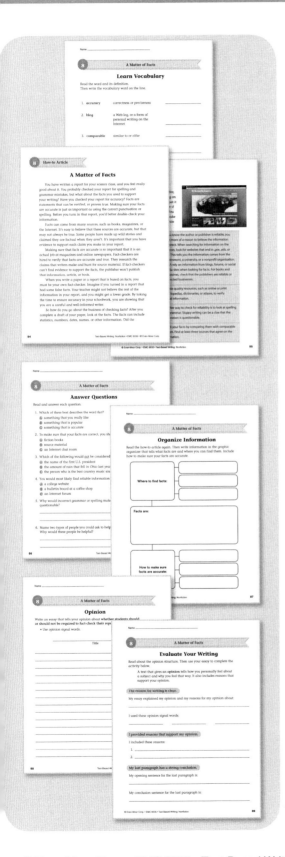

2 Learn Vocabulary

Read aloud each content vocabulary word and have students repeat. Then read aloud and discuss the definitions. Explain that students will have a better understanding of the words after they read the how-to article. Have students write the vocabulary words on the provided lines.

3 Read the How-to Article: *A Matter of Facts*

Read aloud the how-to article as students follow along silently. Then have students reread the article independently or in small groups.

4 Answer Questions About the How-to Article

To ensure reading comprehension, have students answer the text-dependent questions. Review the answers together.

5 Organize Information

Explain to students that they will use an idea-web graphic organizer to help them plan their essays. Guide students in using the text to complete the organizer.

6 Write an Opinion Essay

Have students complete the writing assignment independently, with a partner, or in small groups.

Remind students that an opinion essay:

- tells how you feel about something,
- tells why you feel that way, and
- includes signal words: *I feel, I think, to me, I like, I agree that; I don't like, I disagree that.*

7 Evaluate Your Writing

Explain that students will evaluate their writing to ensure that they have produced well-written essays that follow the opinion structure.

UNIT
8

A Matter of Facts

Unit Focus

You are going to read a how-to article about how facts are used in writing.

As You Read:

Think about where you can best find facts and how to check them for accuracy.

After You Read:

Use information from the article to write an opinion essay about whether students should or should not be required to fact-check their reports.

Lesson Checklist

Check off each task after you complete it.

☐ **Learn Vocabulary**

☐ **Read the How-to Article:** *A Matter of Facts*

☐ **Answer Questions About the How-to Article**

☐ **Organize Information**

☐ **Write an Opinion Essay**

☐ **Evaluate Your Writing**

Learn Vocabulary

Read the word and its definition.
Then write the vocabulary word on the line.

1. **accuracy**   correctness or preciseness   _____

2. **blog**   a Web log, or a form of
                       personal writing on the
                       Internet   _____

3. **comparable**   similar to or alike   _____

4. **double-check**   to check information again;
                       to review   _____

5. **forum**   a place where people can
                       openly discuss thoughts or
                       questions with others   _____

6. **organization**   a group of people who work
                       together for a specific cause   _____

7. **reliable**   consistently good in quality
                       and able to be trusted   _____

8. **statistics**   information represented by
                       numbers; percentages   _____

A Matter of Facts

You have written a report for your science class, and you feel really good about it. You probably checked your report for spelling and grammar mistakes, but what about the facts you used to support your writing? Have you checked your report for accuracy? Facts are statements that can be verified, or proven true. Making sure your facts are accurate is just as important as using the correct punctuation or spelling. Before you turn in that report, you'd better double-check your information.

Facts can come from many sources, such as books, magazines, or the Internet. It's easy to believe that these sources are accurate, but that may not always be true. Some people have made up wild stories and claimed they are factual when they aren't. It's important that you have evidence to support each claim you make in your report.

Making sure that facts are accurate is so important that it is an actual job at magazines and online newspapers. Fact-checkers are hired to verify that facts are accurate and true. They research the claims that writers make and hunt for source material. If fact-checkers can't find evidence to support the facts, the publisher won't publish that information, article, or book.

When you write a paper or a report that is based on facts, you must be your own fact-checker. Imagine if you turned in a report that had some false facts. Your teacher might not believe the rest of the information in your report, and you might get a lower grade. By taking the time to ensure accuracy in your schoolwork, you are showing that you are a careful and well-informed writer.

So how do you go about the business of checking facts? After you complete a draft of your paper, look at the facts. The facts can include statistics, numbers, dates, names, or other information. Did the information come from reliable sources? Remember, anyone can put anything on the Internet and claim that it is true. How do you know if you can trust a source? You can take these steps to make sure your facts are accurate and precise:

Check the author or source of the facts.	If you know the author or publisher is reliable, you have more of a reason to believe the information is correct. When searching for information on the Internet, look for websites that end in *.gov*, *.edu*, or *.org*. This tells you the information comes from the government, a university, or a nonprofit organization. Don't rely on information from blogs, forums, or social media sites when looking for facts. For books and magazines, check that the publishers are reliable or respected businesses.
Use standard sources.	Choose quality resources, such as online or print encyclopedias, dictionaries, or atlases, to verify factual information.
Look for mistakes.	Another way to check for reliability is to look at spelling and grammar. Sloppy writing can be a clue that the information is questionable.
Double-check your facts.	Check your facts by comparing them with comparable sources. Find at least three sources that agree on the information.

Name _____

Answer Questions

Read and answer each question.

1. Which of these best describes the word *fact*?

   Ⓐ something that you really like

   Ⓑ something that is popular

   Ⓒ something that is accurate

2. To make sure that your facts are correct, you should use ____.

   Ⓐ fiction books

   Ⓑ source material

   Ⓒ an Internet chat room

3. Which of the following would <u>not</u> be considered a fact?

   Ⓐ the name of the first U.S. president

   Ⓑ the amount of rain that fell in Ohio last year

   Ⓒ the person who is the best country music singer

4. You would most likely find reliable information on ____.

   Ⓐ a college website

   Ⓑ a bulletin board at a coffee shop

   Ⓒ an Internet forum

5. Why would incorrect grammar or spelling make someone's writing questionable?

   _____

   _____

6. Name two types of people you could ask to help you verify facts. Why would these people be helpful?

   _____

   _____

   Text-Based Writing: Nonfiction • EMC 6035 • © Evan-Moor Corp.

Name _____

Organize Information

Read the how-to article again. Then write information in the graphic organizer that tells what facts are and where you can find them. Include how to make sure your facts are accurate.

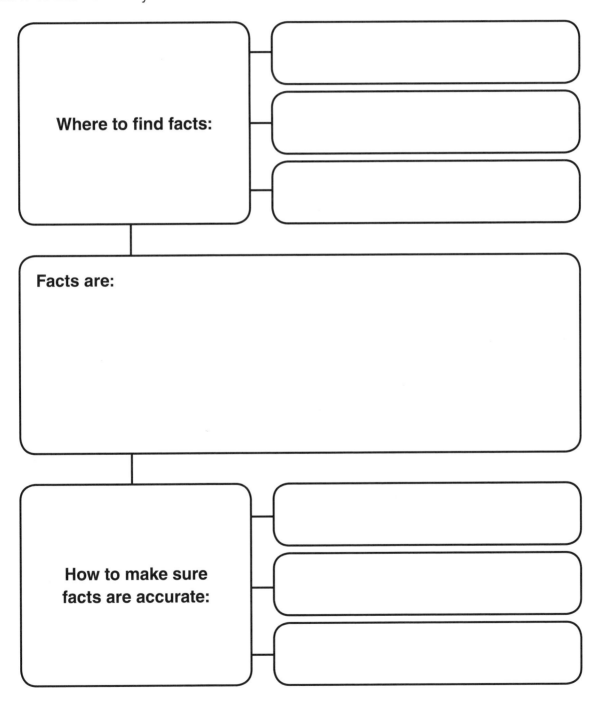

Where to find facts:

Facts are:

How to make sure facts are accurate:

Name _____

Opinion

Write an essay that tells your opinion about **whether students should or should not be required to fact-check their reports.**

- • Use opinion signal words.

_____
Title

_____

_____

_____

_____

_____

_____

_____

_____

_____

_____

_____

_____

_____

_____

Name _____

Evaluate Your Writing

Read about the opinion structure. Then use your essay to complete the activity below.

> A text that gives an **opinion** tells how you personally feel about a subject and why you feel that way. It also includes reasons that support your opinion.

The reason for writing is clear.

My essay explained my opinion and my reasons for my opinion about:

_____

I used these opinion signal words:

_____   _____   _____

I provided reasons that support my opinion.

I included these reasons:

1. _____

2. _____

My last paragraph has a strong conclusion.

My opening sentence for the last paragraph is:

_____

My conclusion sentence for the last paragraph is:

_____

May I Take Your Order?

Lesson Objectives

Writing

Students use information from the health article to write an argument essay.

Vocabulary

Students learn content vocabulary words and use those words to write an argument about whether it is or is not good for people to eat fast food.

Content Knowledge

Students learn the processes and health risks involved with fast food.

Essential Understanding

Students understand that fresh food is a better option for living a long, healthy life.

Prepare the Unit

Reproduce and distribute one copy for each student.

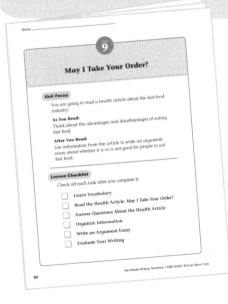

1 Unit Focus and Lesson Checklist

Distribute one unit to each student and direct students' attention to the Unit Focus and Lesson Checklist. Tell them they will be able to refer to the focus of the unit as needed while working on the lessons. Instruct students to check off each task on the checklist after they complete it.

Read aloud the focus statements, and verify that students understand their purpose for reading. Ask:

• *What are we going to read about?* (the fast-food industry)

• *What are you going to learn about it?* (the advantages and disadvantages of eating fast food)

• *What are you going to write based on this article?* (an argument essay)

CCSS: W 5.1, 5.4, 5.8   RIT 5.3, 5.4, 5.10

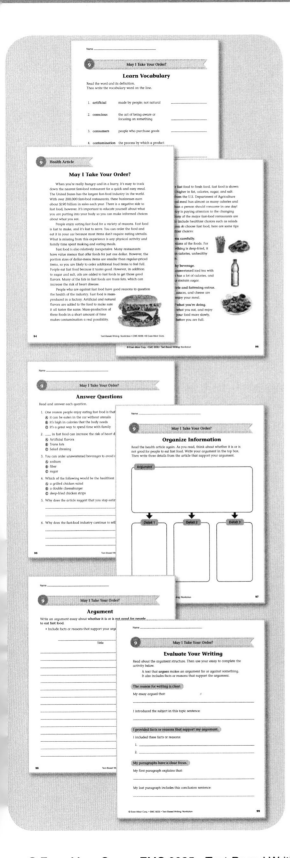

2 Learn Vocabulary

Read aloud each content vocabulary word and have students repeat. Then read aloud and discuss the definitions. Explain that students will have a better understanding of the words after they read the health article. Have students write the vocabulary words on the provided lines.

3 Read the Health Article: *May I Take Your Order?*

Read aloud the health article as students follow along silently. Then have students reread the article independently or in small groups.

4 Answer Questions About the Health Article

To ensure reading comprehension, have students answer the text-dependent questions. Review the answers together.

5 Organize Information

Explain to students that they will use an argument graphic organizer to help them plan their essays. Guide students in using the text to complete the organizer.

6 Write an Argument Essay

Have students complete the writing assignment independently, with a partner, or in small groups.

Remind students that an argument essay:

- makes an argument for or against something,

- gives reasons or facts to support the argument, and

- includes an introductory topic sentence and a conclusion sentence at the end.

7 Evaluate Your Writing

Explain that students will evaluate their writing to ensure that they have produced well-written essays that follow the argument structure.

UNIT 9

May I Take Your Order?

Unit Focus

You are going to read a health article about the fast-food industry.

As You Read:

Think about the advantages and disadvantages of eating fast food.

After You Read:

Use information from the article to write an argument essay about whether it is or is not good for people to eat fast food.

Lesson Checklist

Check off each task after you complete it.

☐ Learn Vocabulary

☐ Read the Health Article: *May I Take Your Order?*

☐ Answer Questions About the Health Article

☐ Organize Information

☐ Write an Argument Essay

☐ Evaluate Your Writing

Learn Vocabulary

Read the word and its definition.
Then write the vocabulary word on the line.

1. **artificial**   made by people; not natural   _____

2. **conscious**   the act of being aware or focusing on something   _____

3. **consumers**   people who purchase goods   _____

4. **contamination**   the process by which a product becomes dangerous, such as when food touches harmful bacteria   _____

5. **heart disease**   a disease that weakens the heart or blocks the normal flow of blood   _____

6. **mass-produced**   created in very large quantities   _____

7. **portion**   the amount of food served to one person   _____

8. **value**   a lower cost or a good deal on a purchase   _____

May I Take Your Order?

When you're really hungry and in a hurry, it's easy to track down the nearest fast-food restaurant for a quick and easy meal. The United States has the largest fast-food industry in the world. With over 200,000 fast-food restaurants, these businesses earn about $190 billion in sales each year. There is a negative side to fast food, however. It's important to educate yourself about what you are putting into your body so you can make informed choices about what you eat.

People enjoy eating fast food for a variety of reasons. Fast food is fast to make, and it's fast to serve. You can order the food and eat it in your car because most items don't require eating utensils. What is missing from this experience is any physical activity and family time spent making and eating meals.

Fast food is also relatively inexpensive. Many restaurants have value menus that offer foods for just one dollar. However, the portion sizes of dollar-menu items are smaller than regular-priced items, so you are likely to order additional food items to feel full. People eat fast food because it tastes good. However, in addition to sugar and salt, oils are added to fast foods to get those good flavors. Many of the fats in fast foods are trans fats, which can increase the risk of heart disease.

People who are against fast food have good reasons to question the health of the industry. Fast food is mass-produced in a factory. Artificial and natural flavors are added to the food to make sure it all tastes the same. Mass-production of these foods in a short amount of time makes contamination a real possibility.

When you compare fast food to fresh food, fast food is shown to be lower in fiber and higher in fat, calories, sugar, and salt. Based on information from the U.S. Department of Agriculture Food Guide, one fast-food meal has almost as many calories and sodium and more fat than a person should consume in one day!

The fast-food industry is paying attention to the changing habits of consumers. Many of the major fast-food restaurants are updating their menus to include healthier choices such as salads and grilled chicken. If you *do* choose fast food, here are some tips to help you make healthier choices:

+ **Look at the menu carefully.**
  Read the descriptions of the foods. For example, if something is deep-fried, it is usually high in calories, unhealthy fats, and sodium.

+ **Choose a healthy beverage.**
  Drink water or unsweetened iced tea with your meal. Soda has a lot of calories, and sweetened drinks contain sugar.

+ **Avoid high-calorie and fattening extras.**
  Salad dressings, sauces, and cheese are unnecessary to enjoy your meal.

+ **Be conscious of what you're doing.**
  Pay attention to what you eat, and enjoy each bite. Chew your food more slowly, and stop eating before you are full.

May I Take Your Order?

Answer Questions

Read and answer each question.

1. One reason people enjoy eating fast food is that ____.

    Ⓐ it can be eaten in the car without utensils

    Ⓑ it's high in calories that the body needs

    Ⓒ it's a great way to spend time with family

2. ____ in fast food can increase the risk of heart disease.

    Ⓐ Artificial flavors

    Ⓑ Trans fats

    Ⓒ Salad dressing

3. You can order unsweetened beverages to avoid consuming too much ____.

    Ⓐ sodium

    Ⓑ fiber

    Ⓒ sugar

4. Which of the following would be the healthiest choice of fast food?

    Ⓐ a grilled chicken salad

    Ⓑ a double cheeseburger

    Ⓒ deep-fried chicken strips

5. Why does the article suggest that you stop eating before you are full?

    _____

    _____

6. Why does the fast-food industry continue to sell unhealthy foods?

    _____

    _____

    _____

May I Take Your Order?

Organize Information

Read the health article again. As you read, think about whether it is or is not good for people to eat fast food. Write your argument in the top box. Then write three details from the article that support your argument.

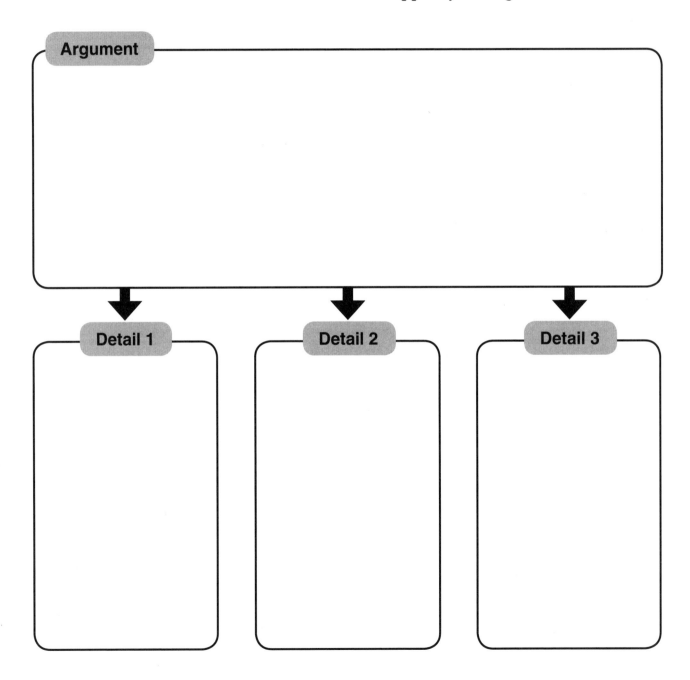

Argument

Detail 1

Detail 2

Detail 3

Name _____

Argument

Write an argument essay about **whether it is or is not good for people to eat fast food.**

• Include facts or reasons that support your argument.

_____
Title

_____

_____

_____

_____

_____

_____

_____

_____

_____

_____

_____

_____

_____

_____

Name _____

Evaluate Your Writing

Read about the argument structure. Then use your essay to complete the activity below.

> A text that **argues** makes an argument for or against something. It also includes facts or reasons that support the argument.

The reason for writing is clear.

My essay argued that:

_____

I introduced the subject in this topic sentence:

_____

I provided facts or reasons that support my argument.

I included these facts or reasons:

1. _____

2. _____

My paragraphs have a clear focus.

My first paragraph explains that:

_____

My last paragraph includes this conclusion sentence:

_____

Lion Lights

Lesson Objectives

Writing
Students use information from the social studies article to write an argument essay.

Vocabulary
Students learn content vocabulary words and use those words to write an argument about whether it is or is not good for Maasai farmers to use Lion Lights.

Content Knowledge
Students learn why the lights were needed and how they are being used today.

Essential Understanding
Students understand that humans need to find nonlethal ways of dealing with nature and protecting our livelihoods.

Prepare the Unit

Reproduce and distribute one copy for each student.

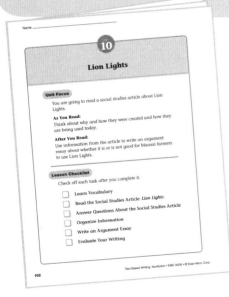

1 Unit Focus and Lesson Checklist

Distribute one unit to each student and direct students' attention to the Unit Focus and Lesson Checklist. Tell them they will be able to refer to the focus of the unit as needed while working on the lessons. Instruct students to check off each task on the checklist after they complete it.

Read aloud the focus statements, and verify that students understand their purpose for reading. Ask:

- *What are we going to read about?* (Lion Lights)

- *What are you going to learn about them?* (why and how they were created and how they are used today)

- *What are you going to write based on this article?* (an argument essay)

CCSS: **W** 5.1, 5.4, 5.8   **RIT** 5.3, 5.4, 5.10

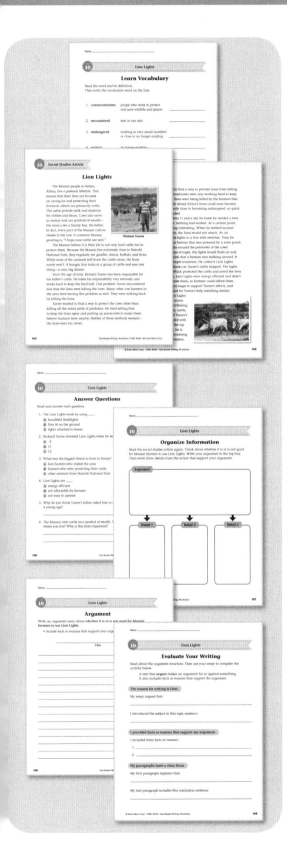

2 Learn Vocabulary

Read aloud each content vocabulary word and have students repeat. Then read aloud and discuss the definitions. Explain that students will have a better understanding of the words after they read the social studies article. Have students write the vocabulary words on the provided lines.

3 Read the Social Studies Article: *Lion Lights*

Read aloud the social studies article as students follow along silently. Then have students reread the article independently or in small groups.

4 Answer Questions About the Social Studies Article

To ensure reading comprehension, have students answer the text-dependent questions. Review the answers together.

5 Organize Information

Explain to students that they will use an argument graphic organizer to help them plan their essays. Guide students in using the text to complete the organizer.

6 Write an Argument Essay

Have students complete the writing assignment independently, with a partner, or in small groups.

Remind students that an argument essay:

- makes an argument for or against something,

- gives reasons or facts to support the argument, and

- includes an introductory topic sentence and a conclusion sentence at the end.

7 Evaluate Your Writing

Explain that students will evaluate their writing to ensure that they have produced well-written essays that follow the argument structure.

UNIT
10

Lion Lights

Unit Focus

You are going to read a social studies article about Lion Lights.

As You Read:

Think about why and how they were created and how they are being used today.

After You Read:

Use information from the article to write an argument essay about whether it is or is not good for Maasai farmers to use Lion Lights.

Lesson Checklist

Check off each task after you complete it.

- [ ] **Learn Vocabulary**
- [ ] **Read the Social Studies Article:** *Lion Lights*
- [ ] **Answer Questions About the Social Studies Article**
- [ ] **Organize Information**
- [ ] **Write an Argument Essay**
- [ ] **Evaluate Your Writing**

Learn Vocabulary

Read the word and its definition.
Then write the vocabulary word on the line.

1. **conservationists**   people who work to protect
                          and save wildlife and plants   _____

2. **encountered**   met or ran into   _____

3. **endangered**   existing in very small numbers
                          or close to no longer existing   _____

4. **extinct**   no longer existing   _____

5. **perimeter**   the outer edges of an area   _____

6. **scarecrows**   human-like objects that are
                          designed to scare away birds
                          or predators from crops or
                          livestock   _____

7. **scholarship**   an amount of free money
                          given to a student to help
                          pay for schooling   _____

8. **solar panel**   equipment that absorbs
                          sunlight and turns it into
                          electricity   _____

Lion Lights

The Maasai people in Kenya, Africa, live a pastoral lifestyle. This means that their lives are focused on caring for and protecting their livestock, which are primarily cattle. The cattle provide milk and material for clothes and shoes. Cows also serve as money and are symbols of wealth— the more cows a family has, the better. In fact, every part of the Maasai culture relates to the cow. A common Maasai greeting is, "I hope your cattle are well."

Richard Turere

The Maasai believe it is their job to not only herd cattle but to protect them. Because the Maasai live extremely close to Nairobi National Park, they regularly see giraffes, rhinos, buffalo, and lions. While most of the animals will leave the cattle alone, the lions surely won't. A hungry lion looks at a group of cattle and sees one thing—a nice, big dinner.

Since the age of nine, Richard Turere has been responsible for his father's cattle. He takes his responsibility very seriously and works hard to keep the herd safe. One problem Turere encountered was that the lions were killing the cows. Many other cow farmers in the area were having this problem as well. They were striking back by killing the lions.

Turere wanted to find a way to protect the cows other than killing off the entire pride of predators. He tried setting fires to keep the lions away and putting up scarecrows to make them believe humans were nearby. Neither of these methods worked— the lions were too clever.

As Turere struggled to find a way to prevent lions from killing his father's cows, conservationists were also working hard to keep the lions safe. So many lions were being killed by the farmers that the conservationists were afraid Africa's lions could soon become extinct. Lions were already close to becoming endangered, so quick action was urgently needed.

By the time Turere was 11 years old, he knew he needed a new approach. Up until now, nothing had worked. At a certain point, Turere realized something interesting. When he walked around at night with a flashlight, the lions would not attack. As an experiment, Turere wired lights to a box with switches. Then he attached the box to a car battery that was powered by a solar panel. He put the lights on poles around the perimeter of the cows' enclosure. In the darkness of night, the lights would flash on and off, making the lions think that a human was walking around. It was a remarkable yet simple invention. He called it Lion Lights.

Immediately, the attacks on Turere's cattle stopped. The lights scared away the lions, which protected the cattle and saved the lives of the lions. In addition, Lion Lights were energy efficient and didn't require a person to operate them, so farmers could afford them. The conservationists were eager to support Turere's efforts, and many other farmers asked for Turere's help installing similar systems. Since then, Lion Lights have been installed all across East Africa and are contributing to the protection of lions, cattle, and farmers. Because of Turere's efforts, he's been rewarded with a scholarship to one of the top schools in Kenya. At 13, he is already on his way to becoming one of Africa's great inventors.

Name _____

Answer Questions

Read and answer each question.

1. The Lion Lights work by using ____.

   Ⓐ handheld flashlights

   Ⓑ fires lit on the ground

   Ⓒ lights attached to boxes

2. Richard Turere invented Lion Lights when he was ____.

   Ⓐ 9

   Ⓑ 11

   Ⓒ 13

3. What was the biggest threat to lions in Kenya?

   Ⓐ lion hunters who visited the area

   Ⓑ farmers who were protecting their cattle

   Ⓒ other animals from Nairobi National Park

4. Lion Lights are ____.

   Ⓐ energy efficient

   Ⓑ not affordable for farmers

   Ⓒ not easy to operate

5. Why do you think Turere's father asked him to care for the cattle at such a young age?

   _____

6. The Maasai view cattle as a symbol of wealth. What is a symbol of wealth where you live? Why is this item important?

   _____

   _____

Organize Information

Read the social studies article again. Think about whether it is or is not good for Maasai farmers to use Lion Lights. Write your argument in the top box. Then write three details from the article that support your argument.

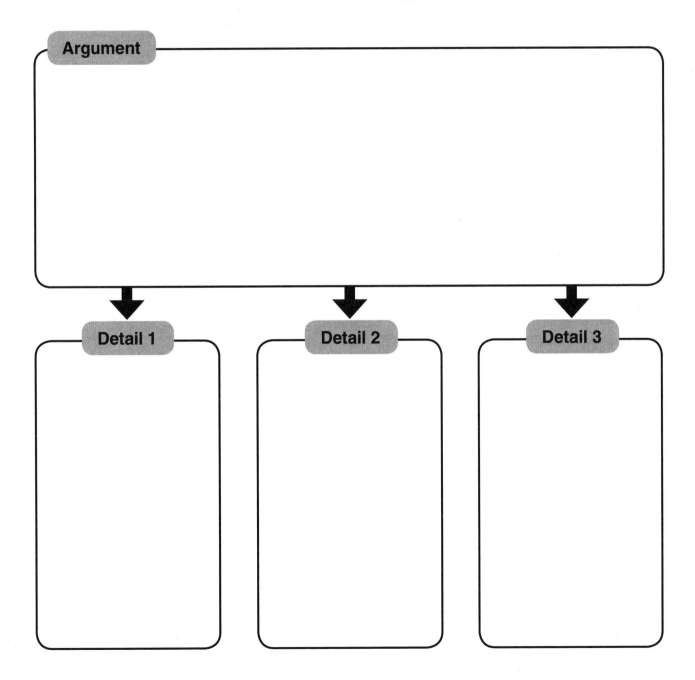

Argument

Detail 1

Detail 2

Detail 3

Name _____

Argument

Write an argument essay about **whether it is or is not good for Maasai farmers to use Lion Lights.**

• Include facts or reasons that support your argument.

_____
Title

_____

_____

_____

_____

_____

_____

_____

_____

_____

_____

_____

_____

Lion Lights

Evaluate Your Writing

Read about the argument structure. Then use your essay to complete the activity below.

> A text that **argues** makes an argument for or against something. It also includes facts or reasons that support the argument.

The reason for writing is clear.

My essay argued that:

_____

I introduced the subject in this topic sentence:

_____

I provided facts or reasons that support my argument.

I included these facts or reasons:

1. _____

2. _____

My paragraphs have a clear focus.

My first paragraph explains that:

_____

My last paragraph includes this conclusion sentence:

_____

One Nation, One Language?

Lesson Objectives

Writing

Students use information from the social studies article to write an argument essay.

Vocabulary

Students learn content vocabulary words and use those words to write about whether all Americans should or should not learn a second language.

Content Knowledge

Students learn why English is not the official language of the U.S. and how many other languages are spoken here.

Essential Understanding

Students understand that learning more than one language will be beneficial to their lives for personal, social, and professional reasons.

Prepare the Unit

Reproduce and distribute one copy for each student.

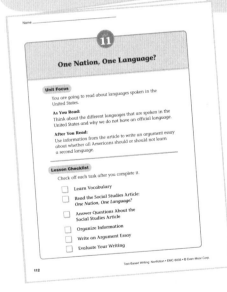

1 Unit Focus and Lesson Checklist

Distribute one unit to each student and direct students' attention to the Unit Focus and Lesson Checklist. Tell them they will be able to refer to the focus of the unit as needed while working on the lessons. Instruct students to check off each task on the checklist after they complete it.

Read aloud the focus statements, and verify that students understand their purpose for reading. Ask:

• *What are we going to read about?* (languages in the U.S.)

• *What are you going to learn about them?* (why English is not the official language)

• *What are you going to write based on this article?* (an argument essay)

CCSS: W 5.1, 5.4, 5.8   RIT 5.3, 5.4, 5.10

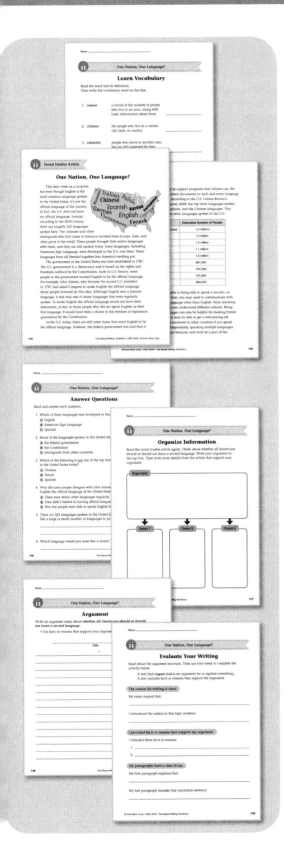

2 Learn Vocabulary

Read aloud each content vocabulary word and have students repeat. Then read aloud and discuss the definitions. Explain that students will have a better understanding of the words after they read the social studies article. Have students write the vocabulary words on the provided lines.

3 Read the Social Studies Article: *One Nation, One Language?*

Read aloud the social studies article as students follow along silently. Then have students reread the article independently or in small groups.

4 Answer Questions About the Social Studies Article

To ensure reading comprehension, have students answer the text-dependent questions. Review the answers together.

5 Organize Information

Explain to students that they will use an argument graphic organizer to help them plan their essays. Guide students in using the text to complete the organizer.

6 Write an Argument Essay

Have students complete the writing assignment independently, with a partner, or in small groups.

Remind students that an argument essay:

- makes an argument for or against something,

- gives reasons or facts to support the argument, and

- includes an introductory topic sentence and a conclusion sentence at the end.

7 Evaluate Your Writing

Explain that students will evaluate their writing to ensure that they have produced well-written essays that follow the argument structure.

Name _____

One Nation, One Language?

Unit Focus

You are going to read about languages spoken in the United States.

As You Read:

Think about the different languages that are spoken in the United States and why we do not have an official language.

After You Read:

Use information from the article to write an argument essay about whether all Americans should or should not learn a second language.

Lesson Checklist

Check off each task after you complete it.

- ☐ **Learn Vocabulary**
- ☐ **Read the Social Studies Article:** *One Nation, One Language?*
- ☐ **Answer Questions About the Social Studies Article**
- ☐ **Organize Information**
- ☐ **Write an Argument Essay**
- ☐ **Evaluate Your Writing**

Learn Vocabulary

Read the word and its definition.
Then write the vocabulary word on the line.

1. **census**   a record of the number of people
who live in an area, along with
basic information about them   _____

2. **citizens**   the people who live in a certain
city, state, or country   _____

3. **colonists**   people who move to another area
but are still governed by their
homeland   _____

4. **Congress**   the group of state representatives
who work to pass or reject laws   _____

5. **democracy**   a system of government in which
the people have voting rights   _____

6. **immigrants** people who move to a new country _____

7. **native
language**   the first language a person
learns   _____

8. **official**   agreed upon by laws or voters   _____

One Nation, One Language?

This may come as a surprise, but even though English is the most common language spoken in the United States, it's not the official language of the country. In fact, the U.S. does not have an official language. Instead, according to the 2010 Census, there are roughly 325 languages spoken here. The colonists and other immigrants who first came to America traveled from Europe, Asia, and other parts of the world. These people brought their native languages with them, and they are still spoken today. Some languages, including American Sign Language, were developed in the U.S. over time. These languages have all blended together into America's melting pot.

The government of the United States was first established in 1787. The U.S. government is a democracy and is based on the rights and freedoms outlined by the Constitution. Early in U.S. history, some people in the government wanted English to be the official language. For example, John Adams, who became the second U.S. president in 1797, had asked Congress to make English the official language. Many people frowned on this idea. Although English was a popular language, it was only one of many languages that were regularly spoken. To make English the official language would not have been democratic, or fair, to those people who did not speak English as their first language. It would have been a threat to the freedom of expression guaranteed by the Constitution.

In the U.S. today, there are still some states that want English to be the official language. However, the federal government has said that if these states ask for money to support programs that citizens use, the states must print all important documents in each and every language spoken by those citizens. According to the U.S. Census Bureau's American Community Survey 2009, the top three languages spoken in the U.S. are English, Spanish, and the Chinese languages. This chart lists just a few of the other languages spoken in the U.S.:

Language	Estimated Number of People
Tagalog (Philippines)	1.5 million+
French	1.3 million
Vietnamese	1.3 million
German	1.1 million
Korean	1.0 million
Russian	881,000
Italian	754,000
Portuguese	731,000
Polish	594,000

There are many benefits to being able to speak a second—or even a third—language. First, you may need to communicate with someone who speaks a language other than English. Next, knowing other languages can help you understand different cultures. Being able to speak other languages can also be helpful for making friends and for travel. Finally, you may be able to get a well-paying job with a company that has locations in other countries if you speak another language. Most importantly, speaking multiple languages allows you to broaden your horizons and truly be a part of the American melting pot.

One Nation, One Language?

Answer Questions

Read and answer each question.

1. Which of these languages was developed in the United States?

   Ⓐ English

   Ⓑ American Sign Language

   Ⓒ Spanish

2. Many of the languages spoken in the United States came from ____.

   Ⓐ the federal government

   Ⓑ the Constitution

   Ⓒ immigrants from other countries

3. Which of the following is not one of the top three languages spoken in the United States today?

   Ⓐ Chinese

   Ⓑ French

   Ⓒ Spanish

4. Why did some people disagree with John Adams when he wanted to make English the official language of the United States?

   Ⓐ There were many other languages regularly spoken at the time.

   Ⓑ They didn't believe in having official languages in any country.

   Ⓒ Very few people were able to speak English back then.

5. There are 325 languages spoken in the United States. Does this seem like a large or small number of languages to you? Why?

   _____

   _____

6. Which language would you most like to learn? Why?

   _____

Name _____

Organize Information

Read the social studies article again. Think about whether all Americans should or should not learn a second language. Write your argument in the top box. Then write three details from the article that support your argument.

Argument

Detail 1

Detail 2

Detail 3

Argument

Write an argument essay about **whether all Americans should or should not learn a second language.**

- • Use facts or reasons that support your argument.

_____

Title

_____

_____

_____

_____

_____

_____

_____

_____

_____

_____

_____

_____

_____

_____

   Text-Based Writing: Nonfiction • EMC 6035 • © Evan-Moor Corp.

Name _____

Evaluate Your Writing

Read about the argument structure. Then use your essay to complete the activity below.

> A text that **argues** makes an argument for or against something. It also includes facts or reasons that support the argument.

The reason for writing is clear.

My essay argued that:

_____

I introduced the subject in this topic sentence:

_____

I provided facts or reasons that support my argument.

I included these facts or reasons:

1. _____

2. _____

My paragraphs have a clear focus.

My first paragraph explains that:

_____

My last paragraph includes this conclusion sentence:

_____

Simple Treats

Lesson Objectives

Writing
Students use information from the social studies article to write an argument essay.

Vocabulary
Students learn content vocabulary words and use those words to write about whether people did or did not benefit from buying and eating simple treats during the Great Depression.

Content Knowledge
Students learn about the difficulties during the Great Depression and how treats were a good, affordable distraction.

Essential Understanding
Students understand that people need simple pleasures during hard times to help them cope.

Prepare the Unit

Reproduce and distribute one copy for each student.

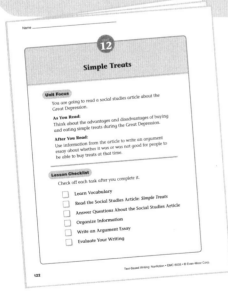

1 Unit Focus and Lesson Checklist

Distribute one unit to each student and direct students' attention to the Unit Focus and Lesson Checklist. Tell them they will be able to refer to the focus of the unit as needed while working on the lessons. Instruct students to check off each task on the checklist after they complete it.

Read aloud the focus statements, and verify that students understand their purpose for reading. Ask:

- *What are we going to read about?* (the Great Depression)

- *What are you going to learn about it?* (the advantages and disadvantages of buying treats at that time)

- *What are you going to write based on this article?* (an argument essay)

CCSS: **W** 5.1, 5.4, 5.8   **RIT** 5.3, 5.4, 5.10

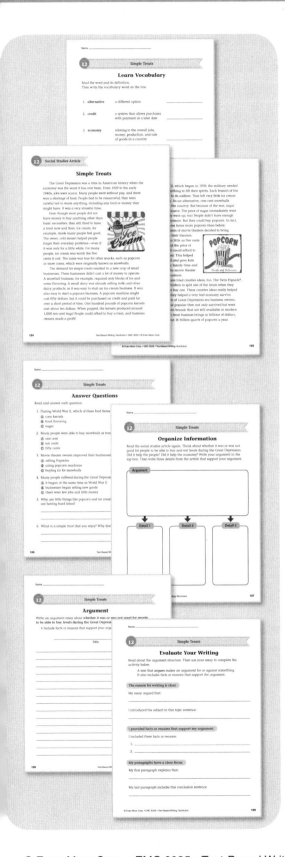

2 Learn Vocabulary

Read aloud each content vocabulary word and have students repeat. Then read aloud and discuss the definitions. Explain that students will have a better understanding of the words after they read the social studies article. Have students write the vocabulary words on the provided lines.

3 Read the Social Studies Article: *Simple Treats*

Read aloud the social studies article as students follow along silently. Then have students reread the article independently or in small groups.

4 Answer Questions About the Social Studies Article

To ensure reading comprehension, have students answer the text-dependent questions. Review the answers together.

5 Organize Information

Explain to students that they will use an argument graphic organizer to help them plan their essays. Guide students in using the text to complete the organizer.

6 Write an Argument Essay

Have students complete the writing assignment independently, with a partner, or in small groups.

Remind students that an argument essay:

- makes an argument for or against something,

- gives reasons or facts to support the argument, and

- includes an introductory topic sentence and a conclusion sentence at the end.

7 Evaluate Your Writing

Explain that students will evaluate their writing to ensure that they have produced well-written essays that follow the argument structure.

UNIT
12

Simple Treats

Unit Focus

You are going to read a social studies article about the Great Depression.

As You Read:

Think about the advantages and disadvantages of buying and eating simple treats during the Great Depression.

After You Read:

Use information from the article to write an argument essay about whether it was or was not good for people to be able to buy treats at that time.

Lesson Checklist

Check off each task after you complete it.

☐ Learn Vocabulary

☐ Read the Social Studies Article: *Simple Treats*

☐ Answer Questions About the Social Studies Article

☐ Organize Information

☐ Write an Argument Essay

☐ Evaluate Your Writing

Simple Treats

Learn Vocabulary

Read the word and its definition.
Then write the vocabulary word on the line.

1. **alternative**   a different option   _____

2. **credit**   a system that allows purchases with payment at a later date   _____

3. **economy**   relating to the overall jobs, money, production, and sale of goods in a country   _____

4. **era**   a period of time or of history that is sometimes measured in decades or centuries   _____

5. **necessities**   things needed for survival; food, shelter, clothing   _____

6. **rationed**   limited or only available in small quantities   _____

7. **scarce**   difficult to find or get; mostly unavailable   _____

Simple Treats

The Great Depression was a time in American history when the economy was the worst it has ever been. From 1929 to the early 1940s, jobs were scarce. Many people went without pay, and there was a shortage of food. People had to be resourceful; they were careful not to waste anything, including any food or money they might have. It was a very stressful time.

Even though most people did not have money to buy anything other than basic necessities, they still liked to have a treat now and then. Ice cream, for example, made many people feel good. The sweet, cold dessert helped people forget their everyday problems—even if it was only for a little while. For many people, ice cream was worth the five

cents it cost. The same was true for other snacks, such as popcorn or snow cones, which were originally known as snowballs.

The demand for simple treats resulted in a new crop of small businesses. These businesses didn't cost a lot of money to operate. A snowball business, for example, required only blocks of ice and some flavoring. A small dairy was already selling milk and other dairy products, so it was easy to start an ice-cream business. It was also easy to start a popcorn business. A popcorn machine might cost fifty dollars, but it could be purchased on credit and paid for over a short period of time. One hundred pounds of popcorn kernels cost about ten dollars. When popped, the kernels produced around 1,000 ten-cent bags! People could afford to buy a treat, and business owners made a profit!

During World War II, which began in 1939, the military needed to send servicemen something to lift their spirits. Each branch of the military sent ice cream to its soldiers. That left very little ice cream for nonmilitary citizens. As an alternative, one-cent snowballs became popular across the country. But because of the war, sugar was rationed, so it was scarce. The price of sugar immediately went up, so the price of candy went up, too! People didn't have enough money to buy candy anymore. But they could buy popcorn. In fact, people began eating three times more popcorn than before.

Because of this, owners of movie theaters decided to bring popcorn machines into their theaters. They sold popcorn for as little as five cents a bag. They also lowered the price of movie tickets so families could afford to go to the movies together. This helped parents feel less stressed and gave kids an opportunity to enjoy family time and a treat. It also helped the movie theater owners increase their business.

Fresh and Delicious

Other business owners tried creative ideas, too. The Twin Popsicle®, for example, allowed children to split one of the treats when they each could not afford to buy one. These creative ideas really helped people feel better, and they helped a very bad economy survive.

Thanks to the efforts of Great Depression-era business owners, many foods that became popular then not only survived but went on to become well-known brands that are still available in modern times. Today, the frozen treat business brings in billions of dollars, and Americans eat about 16 billion quarts of popcorn a year.

Simple Treats

Answer Questions

Read and answer each question.

1. During World War II, which of these food items was rationed?

   Ⓐ corn kernels

   Ⓑ food flavoring

   Ⓒ sugar

2. Many people were able to buy snowballs as treats because they cost ____.

   Ⓐ one cent

   Ⓑ ten cents

   Ⓒ fifty cents

3. Movie theater owners improved their businesses by ____.

   Ⓐ selling Popsicles

   Ⓑ using popcorn machines

   Ⓒ buying ice for snowballs

4. Many people suffered during the Great Depression because ____.

   Ⓐ it began at the same time as World War II

   Ⓑ businesses began selling new goods

   Ⓒ there were few jobs and little money

5. Why are little things like popcorn and ice cream helpful to people who are having hard times?

   _____

   _____

6. What is a simple treat that you enjoy? Why does it make you happy?

   _____

   _____

Name _____

Organize Information

Read the social studies article again. Think about whether it was or was not good for people to be able to buy and eat treats during the Great Depression. Did it help the people? Did it help the economy? Write your argument in the top box. Then write three details from the article that support your argument.

Argument

Detail 1

Detail 2

Detail 3

Name _____

UNIT 12 — **Simple Treats**

Argument

Write an argument essay about **whether it was or was not good for people to be able to buy treats during the Great Depression.**

- Include facts or reasons that support your argument.

_____

Title

_____

_____

_____

_____

_____

_____

_____

_____

_____

_____

_____

_____

_____

Evaluate Your Writing

Read about the argument structure. Then use your essay to complete the activity below.

> A text that **argues** makes an argument for or against something. It also includes facts or reasons that support the argument.

The reason for writing is clear.

My essay argued that:

_____

I introduced the subject in this topic sentence:

_____

I provided facts or reasons that support my argument.

I included these facts or reasons:

1. _____

2. _____

My paragraphs have a clear focus.

My first paragraph explains that:

_____

My last paragraph includes this conclusion sentence:

_____

Answer Key

Unit 1

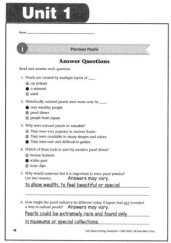

TE Page 16 / SB Page 8

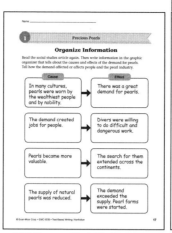

TE Page 17 / SB Page 9

Unit 2

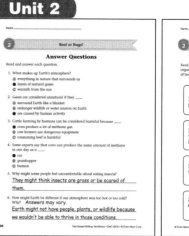

TE Page 26 / SB Page 16

TE Page 27 / SB Page 17

Unit 3

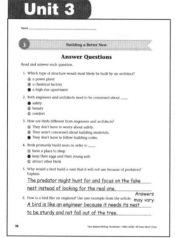

TE Page 36 / SB Page 24

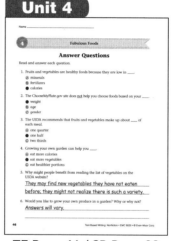

TE Page 37 / SB Page 25

Unit 4

TE Page 46 / SB Page 32

TE Page 47 / SB Page 33

Unit 5

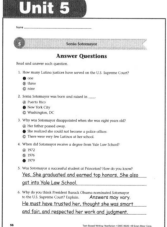

TE Page 56 / SB Page 40

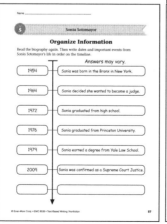

TE Page 57 / SB Page 41

Unit 6

TE Page 66 / SB Page 48

TE Page 67 / SB Page 49

Unit 7

TE Page 76 / SB Page 56

TE Page 77 / SB Page 57

Unit 8

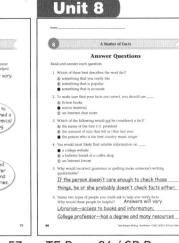

TE Page 86 / SB Page 64

TE Page 87 / SB Page 65

Unit 9

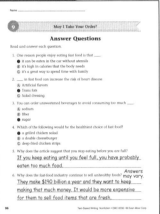

TE Page 96 / SB Page 72

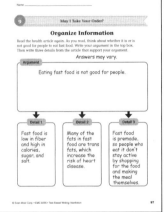

TE Page 97 / SB Page 73

Unit 10

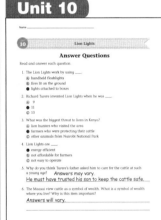

TE Page 106 / SB Page 80

TE Page 107 / SB Page 81

Unit 11

TE Page 116 / SB Page 88

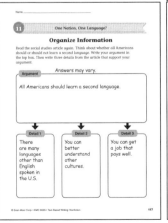

TE Page 117 / SB Page 89

Unit 12

TE Page 126 / SB Page 96

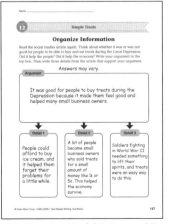

TE Page 127 / SB Page 97

Reading Informational Text

Grade **5**

SAMPLER

Geography Article
Text Structure: Cause and Effect

Earth's Precious Water

Lesson Objective
Students will describe the main steps in the water cycle and explain why it's important for people to conserve water, even though Earth circulates water.

Content Knowledge
Water can be a gas, a liquid, or a solid and can go back and forth from one state to another. The ocean is an important part of the water cycle.

Lesson Preparation

Reproduce and distribute one copy of the article, dictionary page, and activity pages to each student.

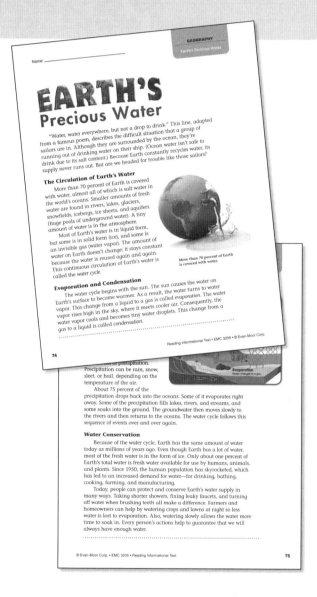

CCSS: RIT 5.1, 5.2, 5.3, 5.4, 5.8   W 5.2, 5.4, 5.9.b

1 Read Aloud the Article

Read aloud *Earth's Precious Water*. Have students follow along silently as you read.

2 Introduce the Vocabulary

Content Vocabulary
Read aloud the Content Vocabulary words and definitions. Point out that three of the four words (*condensation, evaporation,* and *precipitation*) contain the *-tion* suffix. Explain that this suffix changes a verb to a noun that describes an action or condition. Ask students to identify the corresponding verbs for the three words (*condense, evaporate,* and *precipitate*). Discuss definitions and usage as needed.

Academic Vocabulary
Next, read aloud the Academic Vocabulary words and definitions. Discuss definitions and usage as needed. Then read these context sentences from the article, emphasizing the Academic Vocabulary words:

*This continuous **circulation** of Earth's water is called the water cycle.*

*The water cycle follows this **sequence** of events over and over again.*

*Since 1950, the human **population** has **skyrocketed**, which has led to an increased demand for water—for drinking, bathing, cooking, farming, and manufacturing.*

3 Students Read the Article

Have students read the article independently, with a partner, or in small groups. After students read, guide a discussion about the article. Direct students' attention to graphic elements or visual aids.

4 Identify Information

Explain that students will locate important information in the article. After students complete the activity, allow time for a question-and-answer session.

5 Answer Questions

Encourage students to use the article to answer the questions and/or check their answers.

6 Apply Vocabulary

Have students reread the article before they complete the vocabulary activity.

7 Examine Text Structure

Read aloud the Cause and Effect description and Signal Words. Then have students read the article again, underlining signal words in red. Then guide students in completing the activity.

8 Write About It:
The Water Cycle and Conserving Water

Have students complete the writing activity independently or in small groups.

EARTH'S Precious Water

"Water, water everywhere, but not a drop to drink." This line, adapted from a famous poem, describes the difficult situation that a group of sailors are in. Although they are surrounded by the ocean, they're running out of drinking water on their ship. (Ocean water isn't safe to drink due to its salt content.) Because Earth constantly recycles water, its supply never runs out. But are we headed for trouble like those sailors?

The Circulation of Earth's Water

More than 70 percent of Earth is covered with water, almost all of which is salt water in the world's oceans. Smaller amounts of fresh water are found in rivers, lakes, glaciers, snowfields, icebergs, ice sheets, and aquifers (huge pools of underground water). A tiny amount of water is in the atmosphere.

Most of Earth's water is in liquid form, but some is in solid form (ice), and some is an invisible gas (water vapor). The amount of water on Earth doesn't change; it stays constant because the water is reused again and again. This continuous circulation of Earth's water is called the *water cycle*.

More than 70 percent of Earth is covered with water.

Evaporation and Condensation

The water cycle begins with the sun. The sun causes the water on Earth's surface to become warmer. As a result, the water turns to water vapor. This change from a liquid to a gas is called *evaporation*. The water vapor rises high in the sky, where it meets cooler air. Consequently, the water vapor cools and becomes tiny water droplets. This change from a gas to a liquid is called *condensation*.

Precipitation

As more water vapor condenses, the tiny water droplets form clouds. The clouds grow darker and thicker due to more water droplets forming. Eventually, the billions of water droplets become too heavy to stay up in the air any longer. As a result, they fall from the clouds in the form of precipitation. Precipitation can be rain, snow, sleet, or hail, depending on the temperature of the air.

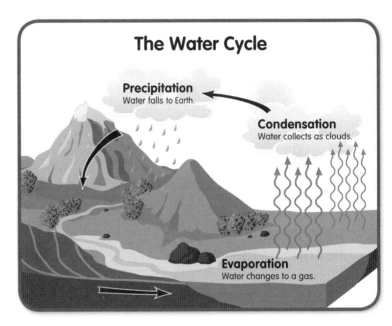

The Water Cycle

Precipitation
Water falls to Earth.

Condensation
Water collects as clouds.

Evaporation
Water changes to a gas.

About 75 percent of the precipitation drops back into the oceans. Some of it evaporates right away. Some of the precipitation fills lakes, rivers, and streams, and some soaks into the ground. The groundwater then moves slowly to the rivers and then returns to the oceans. The water cycle follows this sequence of events over and over again.

Water Conservation

Because of the water cycle, Earth has the same amount of water today as millions of years ago. Even though Earth has a lot of water, most of the fresh water is in the form of ice. Only about one percent of Earth's total water is fresh water available for use by humans, animals, and plants. Since 1950, the human population has skyrocketed, which has led to an increased demand for water—for drinking, bathing, cooking, farming, and manufacturing.

Today, people can protect and conserve Earth's water supply in many ways. Taking shorter showers, fixing leaky faucets, and turning off water when brushing teeth all make a difference. Farmers and homeowners can help by watering crops and lawns at night so less water is lost to evaporation. Also, watering slowly allows the water more time to soak in. Every person's actions help to guarantee that we will always have enough water.

Dictionary

Content Vocabulary

condensation
the process by which a gas becomes a liquid due to a decrease in temperature

evaporation
the process by which a liquid becomes a gas due to an increase in temperature

precipitation
water that falls to the ground as rain, snow, sleet, or hail

water cycle
the series of changes that water naturally undergoes on, above, and below Earth's surface as it circulates through the environment

Academic Vocabulary

circulation
the movement of something through steps in a process

sequence
the order in which related events happen or are supposed to happen

population
the number of people who live in a certain place

skyrocketed
increased rapidly to a very high amount or level

Write a sentence that includes at least one vocabulary word.

_____

_____

Identify Information

Check the box after you complete each task.

		Completed
✎	Highlight the reason that Earth never runs out of water.	☐
★	Put a star by the sentence that states how much of Earth is covered with water.	☐
[ ]	Put brackets around the sentence that tells the three forms of Earth's water.	☐
~	Draw a squiggly line under the sentences that explain the sun's role in the water cycle.	☐
✔	Put a check mark next to the sentence that describes what happens when water vapor cools.	☐
!	Put an exclamation point beside the word that means "water changing from a gas to a liquid."	☐
○	Circle the sentence that describes what happens to precipitation that soaks into the ground.	☐
—	Underline the percentage of Earth's water that living things can use.	☐
▲	Put a triangle beside the year when the total human population started to skyrocket.	☐
☐	Draw boxes around the sentences that tell what people can do to help conserve and protect Earth's water.	☐
?	Put a question mark beside any words or sentences you don't understand.	☐

Name: _____

Answer Questions

Use information from the article to answer each question.

1. As part of the water cycle, water does <u>not</u> change into _____.
   Ⓐ an element
   Ⓑ a liquid
   Ⓒ a gas
   Ⓓ a solid

2. The amount of usable fresh water on Earth is _____.
   Ⓐ more than 70 percent of all of Earth's water
   Ⓑ less than 1 percent of all of Earth's water
   Ⓒ increasing because of precipitation
   Ⓓ decreasing because of evaporation

3. Where is salt water found on Earth, and where is fresh water found?

   _____

   _____

   _____

4. After more and more water droplets form in clouds, what causes them to finally fall?

   _____

   _____

5. How much water is on Earth today compared to millions of years ago? Why?

   _____

   _____

6. According to the article, what are some ways that people can conserve water?

   _____

   _____

   _____

Apply Vocabulary

Use a word from the word box to complete each sentence.

Word Box

precipitation	sequence	population	water cycle
skyrocketed	circulation	evaporation	condensation

1. Our lives depend on the _____ of blood throughout our bodies.

2. During _____, a liquid changes into a gas.

3. The human _____ of the world reached seven billion in 2011.

4. The life cycle of every living thing has a _____ of stages.

5. Evaporation, condensation, and precipitation are three steps in the _____.

6. During _____, a gas changes into a liquid.

7. Air temperature determines the form that _____ takes.

8. The number of people on Earth has _____ since 1950.

Cause and Effect

A text that has a **cause-and-effect** structure includes a description of the cause and the resulting effects.

Authors use these signal words to create a **cause-and-effect** structure:

Signal Words

allow	therefore	because of	for this reason
if…then	effects of	as a result of	may be due to
causing	in order to	consequently	which has led to

1. What cause-and-effect relationship about Earth's water supply is explained in the first paragraph?

   _____

   _____

2. The text under the third heading explains the cause-and-effect relationship between temperature and _____.

3. Write two sentences from the article that use **cause-and-effect** signal words.

   a. _____

   _____

   b. _____

   _____

4. How does this text structure help you understand the author's purpose(s)?

   _____

   _____

   _____

   _____

Write About It

Describe the main steps in the water cycle. Then explain why it's important for people to conserve water, even though Earth is always circulating water. Include details from the article in your answer.

The Water Cycle and Conserving Water

_____

_____

_____

_____

_____

_____

_____

_____

_____

_____

_____

_____

_____

_____

_____

_____

_____

_____